Sketching
USER EXPERIENCES

Saul Greenberg
Sheelagh Carpendale
Nicolai Marquardt
Bill Buxton

AMSTERDAM • BOSTON • HEIDELBERG • LONDON
NEW YORK • OXFORD • PARIS • SAN DIEGO
SAN FRANCISCO • SINGAPORE • SYDNEY • TOKYO

ELSEVIER

Morgan Kaufmann Publishers is an imprint of Elsevier

3 THE SINGLE IMAGE 67

Your typical sketch will capture a single moment in time, usually as a single scene in your envisioned user experience. While we won't teach you how to be an artist, we will show you a variety of methods to create these sketches.

4 SNAPSHOTS OF TIME: THE VISUAL NARRATIVE 145

What makes interaction design unique is that it imagines a person's behavior as they interact with a system over time. Storyboards capture this element of time as a series of discrete images that visually narrate what is going on scene by scene.

Books come about in odd ways. This one resulted from serendipity.

Several years ago, **Bill Buxton** decided to aggressively advocate design as fundamental to how companies should develop software for people to use. The problem, he realized, is that most interaction designers (and their managers as well) are not trained as designers. His solution was to write a book *Sketching the User Experience*, where he advocated sketching as a simple way for people to start thinking about the design process. He then pressed this message to academics and practitioners through an aggressive speaking tour, and by influencing Microsoft staff via his job as Principle Researcher at Microsoft Research.

Somewhat at the same time, **Saul Greenberg** was teaching an introductory course on Human Computer Interaction. His concern was that his students would typically start programming the first thing they thought of. Since coding is labour intensive, they often stuck with their initial idea. Most produced variations of traditional designs. A few did add creative aspects to their works, but when they started running usability studies, those aspects invariably suffered from usability problems and were discarded. This wasn't because their ideas were fundamentally bad; they just weren't very well thought out. So Greenberg started a new course that emphasized design over usability, done in the form of a limited design studio. Students were given unfamiliar technologies and ask to create interesting concepts around those technologies. Their first deliverables were a series of sketches, where they had to produce and present many different ideas. They were not allowed to commit to any idea until they explored the design space. Yet almost universally, most students were concerned about their lack of sketching skills, typically saying 'I can't draw'. Consequently, Greenberg started emphasizing a few simple sketching methods suitable for non-artists.

It turns out that Bill and Saul are also outdoor enthusiasts, where they back-country ski and mountain bike together a few times a year. During their trips, they would chat (occasionally) about their work. Saul really liked Bill's book, but thought that it didn't have quite enough on the 'how-to' side. It was one thing to get people to want to engage in design, but quite another to give them the skills to actually get started. Bill really liked Saul's exercises, but thought it needed intellectual framing. Thus the concept of this Workbook emerged, where it would be a 'how-to' sequel to Bill's book. While each book could stand by itself, the two would work best as companions.

Also at the same time, **Sheelagh Carpendale** – who together with Saul started the Interactions Laboratory at the University of Calgary – was somewhat disgruntled by the divide between the University encouraging cross-discipline activities vs. the near impossibility of having non-Computer Scientists accepted to a traditional computer science program. She created the Computational Media Design program, where students from various backgrounds – arts, design, music, computer science – could pursue graduate work at the union / intersection of Computer Science, Art, and Design.

Sheelagh's background began as a professional artist, and then shifted directions into Computer Science. It was only natural that she would come on board as an author, where she would not only bring her dual backgrounds into play, but also her thoughts about how to engage people from different disciplines into the process of design and sketching.

Nicolai Marquardt, a PhD graduate student of Saul's, was observing all this from the periphery. Trained as a Diplom (Masters) student at Bauhaus University Germany in the Media Systems program under Professor Tom Gross, he was experienced in both design and hard-core computer science. Sketching was a way of life for him, and a natural part of how he thought as an user experience designer. He not only had a huge amount of experience sketching 'in the wild', but often collected other people's sketches for inspiration. So we asked him to join us, and we became a foursome.

The best way to summarize the above is that all authors are passionate about design thinking as a way to craft the user experience, and about sketching as a way to start thinking as a designer. This book is our attempt to give you the tools to sketch, and thus to design, your own user experiences.

The Sketches in This Preface

Are you experiencing a sinking feeling looking at the sketches of the four authors in this preface? While far from high art, you may think sketches like these are beyond your abilities. Like most people, it could be that the last drawing you did was in Grade 5.

Don't lose heart. These sketches were actually made by one of the authors who has – to be frank – quite pathetic artistic skills. He used a method called *photo traces* to quickly generate these sketches, where he simply traced over existing photographs. We'll introduce you to photo tracing and many other methods that you – the non-artist – can use to generate your own passable sketches.

Acknowledgments

Books like these go well beyond the authors.

- Annie Tat was our original layout designer. She sketched and crafted multiple designs, and produced an exemplar chapter whose look would be applied to all subsequent chapters.

- June Au Yeung and Lindsay MacDonald tranformed our rough drafts – raw text and images – into this layout. They were the ones in the trenches, where both worked hard at tuning each chapter's layout to fit our material, and at responding to all the other chores given to them.

- The students in the Interactions Laboratory at the University of Calgary were a constant source of inspiration: sketching and designing was fundamental to how they produced beautiful systems. We learned from them, and we use some of their work as examples in this book.

- More broadly, the HCI community and the Design community are an incredible intellectual source. We don't pretend to have invented all the methods in this book. We read many articles and books that spoke about sketching and design. We cruised the web and saw wonderful examples of sketches and videos that people had made. We looked at other educators' web sites to see how they taught design. We spoke to colleagues and professionals, and soaked in their knowledge.

We thank all those involved in this book – either directly or indirectly – profusely.

Section 1

Getting into the Mood

Let's get into the sketching mood. What is a user experience? Why is sketching a good way for you to think about and generate user experiences? Why do so many designers carry a sketchbook, and why should you join them? How can you begin sketching to brainstorm and refine your design ideas?

MISSION

To give you, the novice to intermediate user experience designer, step-by-step instructions on a variety of sketching techniques.

WHAT THIS BOOK IS ABOUT

Sketching has long been a best practice for designers. Through sketches, designers follow a generative process of developing, honing, and choosing ideas. Designers also use sketches to discuss, exchange and critique ideas with others.

User experience designers are a special breed of designer, for they focus on creating a user experience that unfolds over time. Thus their design sketches need to incorporate the actions, interactions, and changes of this experience across time. In this workbook, we use step-by-step instructions to teach various sketching methods that capture this time element. Collectively, these methods will be your sketching repertoire: a toolkit where you can choose the method most appropriate for expressing your design idea.

Our hope is that you, the user experience designer, will learn these methods with other workmates, which in turn will help you cultivate a culture of experience-based design in your workplace.

COMPANION BOOK

You can use this workbook as is. However, you will get even more out of it if you read Bill Buxton's book: *Sketching User Experiences: Getting the Design Right and the Right Design*, Morgan Kaufmann (2007). That book is somewhat more theoretical, and will get you thinking about *why* you should sketch, while this workbook serves as a how-to guide to actual sketching methods.

You don't have to read Buxton's book, as we summarize his main points in Chapter 1.2. While we still recommend his book for its deeper background and discussions (and because it is also fun to read!), our summary should get you into the right frame of mind.

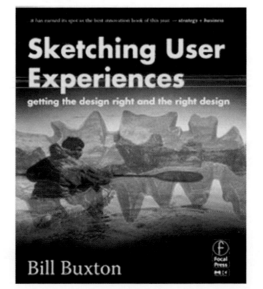

WHY SKETCH?

When you learn and apply these sketching techniques to your daily design practice, the act of sketching will help you:

- think more openly and creatively about your ideas;
- create abundant ideas without worrying about their quality;
- invent and explore concepts by being able to record ideas quickly;
- record ideas that you come across;
- discuss, critique, and share ideas with others;
- choose ideas worth pursuing;
- archive your ideas for later reflection;
- have fun creating while designing.

Doing Rather Than Reading

Reading about a sketching technique is different from actually doing the technique. In this workbook, we choose examples that encourage you to do these sketching techniques as you read about them.

- The examples we use to illustrate the sketch method are deliberately trivial, so that the focus is on the sketching technique rather than on the interface being created.
- The sketched examples are designed to be easy to reproduce.
- The instructions are supported with rich graphical layouts and photographic images to provide visual references and to make the steps more memorable.
- The chosen sketching techniques are inexpensive. The materials and tools required to do a particular technique are commonly available, well documented, and have a reasonably low learning curve.

AUDIENCE

You, the Reader

You are likely a person who wants to learn, understand, practice and even teach experience design. This includes all professionals, amateurs, and students with interests in user experience design, interaction design, interface design and information architecture, but who have not been trained within a conventional design discipline. It also includes designers who do have such training, but who have not specifically practiced the time element that is so critical to interactive interfaces. Regardless of your background, little prior experience is required: anyone can learn these methods.

You, the Learner

Your community will affect how you learn and practice these sketching methods. You may be:

- an individual practitioner of interaction design, where you are developing and/or supplementing your own skills;
- a group of people (e.g., an interface design team) who are self-teaching and acquiring experience methods collectively, perhaps over one or more informal bag lunch sessions;
- an attendee of a formal professional training program, e.g., put on by a company to promote ongoing skill acquisition, and perhaps to help create a design-oriented culture within that company;
- a student in a university, college or high school class on interaction design, where your instructor is mixing theoretical lectures with practical sketching assignments.

You, the Bad Artist

The methods in this book do not require high or even intermediate levels of artistic skills. As you will see, the very best sketches are sometimes just rough line drawings.

STRUCTURE OF THIS BOOK

We categorize different sketching techniques into sections. We begin with some motivation on why you should sketch, and introduce the sketchbook as your most basic resource. We then introduce methods that let you gather ideas from the real world, where these ideas can inspire how you think as a designer. We continue with sections devoted to sketching methods. These are ordered primarily by the temporal characteristic of a sketch: from sketching a single moment in time, to illustrating snapshots of interactive activities over time, to animating continuous sequences. We end by showing you several ways that you can involve others in your sketching process, where their reactions and feedback can provide valuable insight into how your ideas could be improved. Sections are progressive, where we layer and build upon concepts presented in previous sections.

Sections contain chapter modules that in turn contain a particular idea or sketching method. In each module, we explain how the idea or method should be used, and describe, illustrate, and annotate all its key steps. Each module describes what special materials and tools are needed (if any), steps on how to set up the sketch, and how to do the sketch. The how-to instructions are also supported with tips and hints.

The workbook also practices what we preach. Each chapter is richly illustrated with many sketches, all which we created using the various sketch methods introduced in this book. Look at them for further inspiration.

Enjoy!

Sketching User Experiences
getting the design right and the right design

Bill Buxton

Why Should I Sketch? | 1.2

a synopsis of Buxton's Sketching
User Experiences: Getting the Design
Right and the Right Design

Why sketch? Why should you care? Why should you even bother to learn sketching skills? Bill Buxton, one of the authors of this workbook, answered these questions in his 2007 /book: **Sketching User Experiences: Getting the Design Right and the Right Design**. We do recommend you read that book – it's engaging, fun, and chock-full of good advice.

This chapter is for those who haven't read the book, or who need a reminder of what that book is about. It is a synopsis of Bill's argument about why you and your organization should care about sketching.

SKETCHING IS ABOUT DESIGN

Sketching is not about drawing. Rather, it is about design. Primarily, it is:

- a fundamental tool that helps designers express, develop and communicate design ideas;
- a critical part of a process that begins with idea generation, to design elaboration, to design choices, and ultimately to engineering.

GETTING THE DESIGN RIGHT

Getting the design right is about starting with a single design idea – usually the first idea you generate (left figure), and then continually evolving, improving, and developing it (right figure). As seen in the figure, we can think of the design space of an idea as a 3D hill. The best possible design of the idea is at the hill's peak, and other lesser designs are below. The goal is to discover the optimal design solution for that idea, ie, to get as close to the peak as possible. This is iterative design, and how most engineers and software developers are trained to think about design.

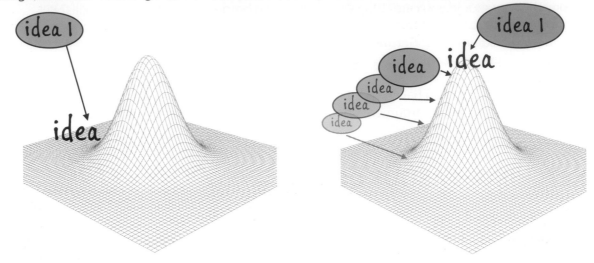

The Problem

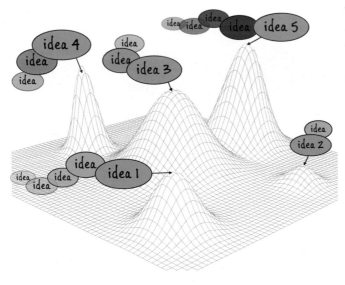

The problem is that the above design can only be as good as that particular idea. If the idea is not a good one, then the 'best' design solution will only be so-so. Consider the figure on the right, which envisages how other design ideas may have fared in the design space.

No matter how hard you work on that first idea, you won't get to other potentially better ideas. The point is that if you consider many ideas rather than a single one, you may find a better overall solution. Computer Scientists even have a name for this problem: **local hill climbing**, where the local maxima is potentially much less than the optimal (the global) maxima.

To illustrate, consider cell phone design. For years, cell phones were based on the design idea of a physical keyboard and screen. They evolved considerably. Yet it was a different idea – the cell phone with a touch display and no physical keyboard – that radically moved cell phone design into a new direction and created a new market.

GETTING THE RIGHT DESIGN

Getting the Right Design is about considering many other ideas and then choosing between them (see figure below, left). That is:

– generate many ideas, e.g., inspired by brainstorming, discussions, lateral thinking, client discussions, observations of end users, etc.;

– reflect on all your ideas;

– choose the ones that look most promising and develop those in parallel;

– add in new ideas as they come up.

The right figure illustrates this process as a tree, where *multiple solutions* are developed, and choices made about which of the one or more branches – ideas – are worth following.

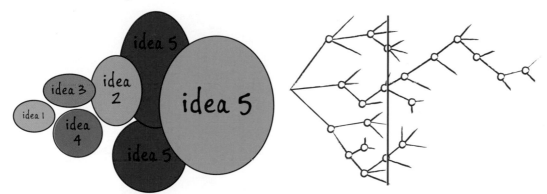

ELABORATION AND REDUCTION

Paul Laseau (1980) had another way to look at this, where he described the design process as a symbiotic relationship between idea *elaboration* and idea *reduction*.

• **Elaboration**: generate solutions. These are the opportunities.

• **Reduction**: decide on the ones worth pursuing, and then elaborate on those solutions.

As a designer, you elaborate to expand your repertoire of ideas, while at the same time reducing the number of ideas – ultimately to the one that is most promising.

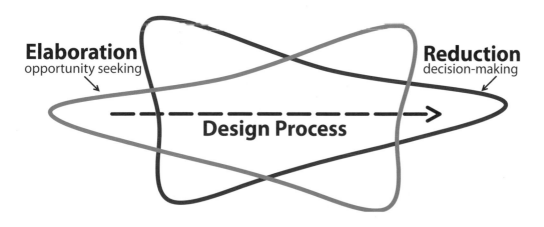

Elaboration
opportunity seeking

Reduction
decision-making

Design Process

THE DESIGN FUNNEL

Stuart Pugh (1990) illustrated elaboration and reduction as a **design funnel**. Of importance is that the generation of ideas and the convergence of ideas alternate, with the process gradually converging to the final concept. As a funnel:

–   each stage is iterative, where one constantly generates and reduces ideas until resolution;

–   the granularity of idea exploration and development is (usually) finer as these iterations progress.

Initial ideas may explore extremely different concept designs at a very high and coarse level. The next stage may explore significant variations of these ideas. Further stages may try to clarify design issues where ideas are explored at finer granularity, until resolution is reached. Of course new radically different ideas may emerge at any time, and should be incorporated.

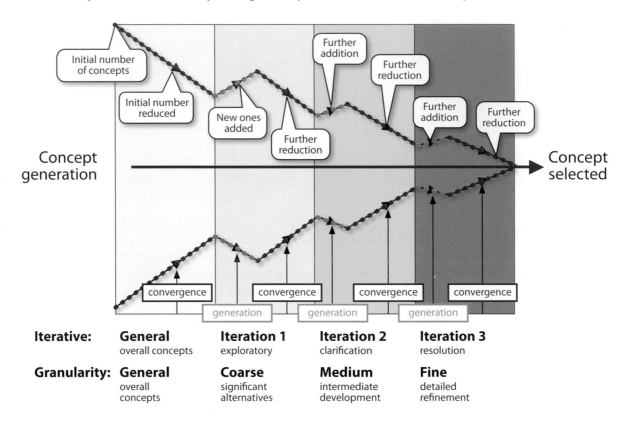

Iterative:	General overall concepts	Iteration 1 exploratory	Iteration 2 clarification	Iteration 3 resolution
Granularity:	General overall concepts	Coarse significant alternatives	Medium intermediate development	Fine detailed refinement

THE PRODUCT VIEW

Let us now consider the importance of design in the software product life cycle. The 'status quo' is that product ideas are judged right at the start, where they are stopped (**red light**) or given the go-ahead (**green light**). If a green light, they go directly to engineering where the product is built. The next phase is when it ships – usually late, with bugs, over budget, and missing functionality.

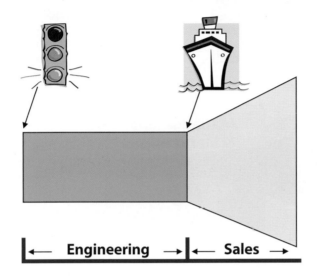

By inserting an explicit design process prior to the green light, many designs can be considered before any commitment is made. The design funnel generates and develops ideas in parallel, where it filters and eliminates designs until convergence. At that point one or more designs can be considered for green light.

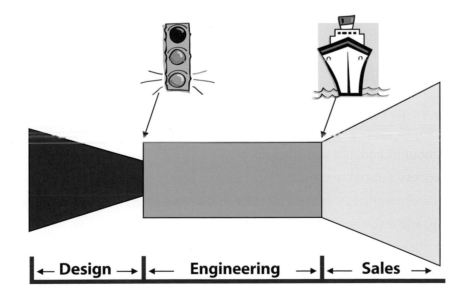

Perhaps a more accurate picture is shown below, as it shows the interplay between design, engineering, management, marketing and sales throughout the entire product cycle. That is, engineers, managers and marketers will work with designers on the early stage, while designers still keep a hand in the process during engineering and sales (perhaps to fix some problems as they occur, or to spark the next generation of this product).

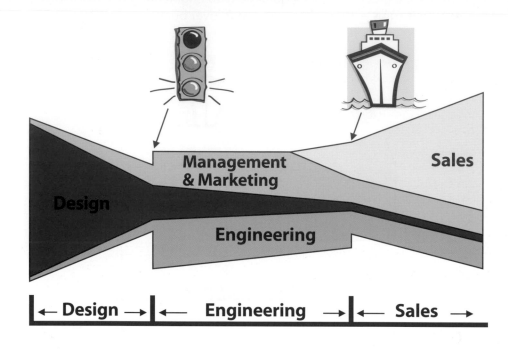

References

Buxton, B. (2007) *Sketching User Experiences: Getting the Design Right and the Right Design*. Morgan Kaufmann.

Laseau, P. (1980) *Graphic Thinking for Architects & Designers*. John Wiley and Sons.

Pugh, S. (1990) *Total Design: Integrated Methods for Successful Products Engineering*. Addison-Wesley. p. 75.

YOU NOW KNOW

Why sketch? Why should you care? Why should you even bother to learn sketching skills? You now know the answers.

1. Sketching is about design, not just drawing.
2. The design process is about getting the right design, and then getting that design right.
3. The design funnel describes this as an interplay between elaboration and reduction
   - generating and elaborating designs;
   - choosing and reducing between designs.
4. Design in product development is about
   - using the design funnel to develop ideas;
   - then considering the best one for green/red light appraisal.

Materials

- sketchbook of your choice

- pencil

- eraser

The regular use of a **sketchbook** is perhaps the most prevalent best practice found across all design disciplines. Many designers keep a sketchbook with them at all times. They use it to record and elaborate their ideas as they come to mind, to gather ideas, notes or artifacts of interest as they see them (especially those that may inspire future ideas), to 'doodle' half-formed thoughts, and to share ideas with others by showing particular sketches.

The sketchbook is particularly valuable as it encourages its owners to collect and develop a multitude of ideas and choose between them, rather than to fixate on a single idea. As explained previously this process of distilling between many ideas is **getting the right design**, whereas the process of developing a particular idea (e.g., through iterative refinement or usability engineering) is **getting the design right**. The former emphasizes design that chooses between idea alternatives, while the later is the creative engineering that refines a particular idea.

WHY A SKETCHBOOK?

Real progress in developing yourself as an interaction designer will depend on you frequently and habitually sketching out your ideas and their variations, recording other people's ideas you may see, reflecting and choosing between these ideas, and then further developing those ideas that seem promising. The sketchbook records all these. Carrying the sketchbook with you at all times will help you incorporate sketching and reflection into your daily routines.

USES OF A SKETCHBOOK

Sketchbooks are useful in many ways. It is a place where you should:

- Jot down and annotate your own initial ideas – and there is no such thing as a bad idea!

- Explore and refine ideas both in the large and in the small.

- Develop variations, alternatives and details.

- Refer back to your ideas and reflect on how your thought processes have changed over time.

- Record other good ideas you see elsewhere, e.g., in other systems, in your readings, and in your colleagues' work.

- Collect existing materials (e.g., pictures from magazines, screen snapshots) and tape them into the sketchbook.

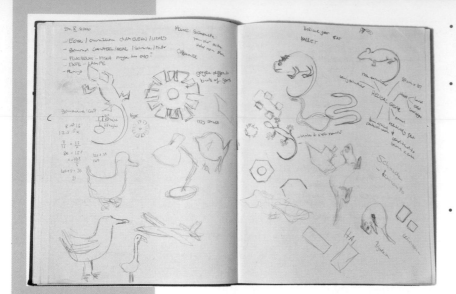

- Develop your skills, your accuracy and your confidence in sketching out your ideas through regular use.

- Be ready to explain them. Sketches do not have to be pretty, beautiful, or even immediately understandable by others. However, you should be able to explain your sketches and ideas when anyone asks about them.

- Use it as an archive. Designers often keep their filled-in sketchbooks for years. You never know when an 'old' idea will come in handy.

BEST PRACTICES

- Always carry your sketchbook with you everywhere (a second small sketchbook is helpful). Jot down ideas as you think about them.

- Always have a pencil handy.

- Sketch frequently, e.g., at least several times a day.

- Fill pages with a series of related drawings about a design idea, or with a single well-composed design idea.

- Consider alternatives (getting the right design). A series of sketches related to the same interaction problem might explore different aspects of the interface. These could include different interface representations, different interaction details, different screens, different levels of details, different contexts of use, and so on. Each page can become a series of studies that will help you develop and reflect on the many ideas you will have.

- Consider details (getting the design right). Follow through on a sketch that captures the essence of a design with more detailed sketches that elaborate on its nuances.

- Annotate drawings appropriately, including information such as descriptions for ideas that you cannot draw out well; textual addendum; sources of your ideas (e.g., books, magazines, collaborators, classmates), creation date, and any other relevant information.

- Do not erase ideas because they are messy or because you no longer like them. Your sketchbook is a record of all your developing ideas, good and bad, not just of your final work.

- The sketchbook is for design only – do not use it for other things just because you do not have any paper.

PROPERTIES OF GOOD SKETCHBOOKS

There are myriads of sketchbooks available, most at reasonable cost. While the choice of sketchbook is personal, there are some properties that make some sketchbook preferable to others.

Buy a nice sketchbook so you can take pride in it. Many designers consider the sketchbook the 'badge' of their profession! Hard covers are far more durable than soft covers, but are somewhat thicker and heavier. Sketchbooks come in either coiled or sewn bound and there are advantages and disadvantages to both. Pages can rip out of cheaper coil bindings. However, coil bindings will let you completely fold over your sketch book so that only one page is in view, which is handy when space is tight. A sewn bound book is more durable, but most do not let yet you fold it over.

Tip

The paper style (grid, textured, plain) is very much a personal preference. As you use your sketchbook, you will discover what paper style works best for you.

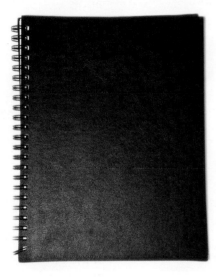

Coiled Binding
Semi-Hard Cardboard Cover

Sewn Binding
Hard Cover

grid paper

plain paper

textured paper

Sketchbooks also come in various sizes. 8½" x 11" or 9" x 12" are typical, and well-suited for most sketches you may make. However, a large sketchbook is of little use to you if you don't have it with you at all times. Thus you may want to keep several sketchbooks of different sizes: a larger one to keep in your pack or briefcase, and a smaller one that fits in your handbag or pocket. Paper thickness also affects portability. Better sketchbooks have thicker paper (which is nicer to draw on), but adds bulk. If you are uncertain about these trade-offs, the key to your choice is to choose at least one sketchbook with a form factor that guarantees you will always have it with you.

Note

Pencils come in different darkness, and felt pens come in different nib thickness. Both are often purchasable as a set. Having a set available can help you emphasize or mute different parts of your drawing, perhaps to show what parts of your idea are more certain versus those that are more speculative.

DRAWING MATERIALS

A sketchbook is of little use without something you can draw with. While there are many drawing tools available, you should – at the very least – always carry a pencil or two with you. Pencil leads vary considerably, with 3B being the most popular (see sidebar). Pens should be avoided unless you are practiced with them: they don't allow you to vary the thickness or blackness of your sketching marks. Other drawing tools can help you add richness and accuracy to your sketches: erasers, pencil sets,

pencil set

felt pen set

colored pencils, markers, paints, charcoal, rulers, compasses, French curves, and so on. Glue and tape will let you paste in material you generated or gathered elsewhere. These are all less portable, but you can always keep them at your normal place of work.

However, remember that a sketch is primarily about recording and elaborating an idea – you can easily get carried away with making a sketch too pretty or accurate. This is why the pencil is your most important sketching tool. Think about keeping a few basic tools with you at all times, and a richer collection of tools in your usual work space. Experiment! Try different tools and see how they influence your idea sketches.

YOU NOW KNOW

A sketchbook is a designer's most fundamental tool. Through it, you can capture and elaborate ideas as they come to you, and review and reflect on them later. Yet a sketchbook can only help you if you carry it with you, and get in the habit of using it. Make it one of your 'best practices'.

The **design funnel** describes a process that you, as an interaction designer, need to habitually apply whenever you think about design problems. This won't happen if you just read about it. You need to do it. As a warm-up to this book, this chapter introduces the **10 plus 10 method** to help you descend into the design funnel. It is more than just an exercise: you should repeat this method as much as possible over design problems that you encounter.

We include three design challenges below as a starting point for you to apply this method, where we provide a worked 'solution' to the first challenge. We deliberately chose challenges that demand novel solutions: it is sometimes harder to generate ideas when existing solutions exist, as they tend to limit how we think about the possible solution space.

THE 10 PLUS 10 METHOD

1. **State your design challenge.**
   It may be framed as a particular problem you want to solve, or around a need stated by a client, or even just as a desire to build a novel system that takes advantage of a new technology.

2. **Generate 10 or more different design concepts of a system that addresses this challenge.**
   This is akin to brainstorming. Your goal is to be as creative and diverse as possible, where you generate many initial concepts. Don't try to judge the merits of these concepts; the important thing is to quickly generate as many as possible. While we will describe sketching methods in later chapters, just do the best you can for now. Try to sketch your concepts as quick drawings, but feel free to annotate them or to accompany them with descriptive text as needed. Your sketches can be quite crude: don't worry about how beautiful or ugly your sketch is.

3. **Reduce the number of design concepts.**
   Review your concepts, where you discard those that don't seem to have much merit. For those that remain, use your sketchbook to show and explain your design(s) to others. Of course, feel free to go back to step 1, where you generate more ideas, and reduce them as needed.

4. **Choose the most promising design concept(s) as a starting point.**
   You will know which concept – or handful of concepts – are the most exciting and promising by how you think about them, how you present them to others, and how others react.

5. **Produce 10 details and/or variations of a particular design concept.**
Using your sketchbook, explore the concept. First, try to generate different ways of realizing that particular concept. Second, go a bit deeper into a particular concept, where you try to flesh out details of your idea.

6. **Present your best idea(s) to a group.**
For example, offer to buy your colleagues coffee and donuts during a coffee break, where the cost of admission is to hear you present your idea. Solicit feedback from them. At this early stage, tell your audience that the best feedback they can give will be suggestions about possible redesigns.

7. **As your ideas change, sketch them out.**
Continue to refine and generate your concept as needed.

DESIGN CHALLENGE 1: CONNECTING TWO SMART PHONES

1

The Design Challenge
There are many cases when you may want to connect your mobile smart phone to a nearby person's smart phone, for example, to exchange information such as photos and contacts. While the network infrastructure is there for one phone to detect and connect to other nearby phones (e.g., via Bluetooth), security requires that people somehow authenticate that connection through some initial sequence as there may be many people with smart phones within range. This usually involves dialog boxes, cryptic requests, and other demands on people that make this both tedious and difficult.

For this exercise, brainstorm 10 novel ways that two people can connect two mobile devices together that do not demand these painful dialogs.

Assumptions
- Your mobile device detects all phones in nearby range and can communicate to them in a limited manner.
- You and the person you want to connect can perform some action that both phones recognize as a 'handshake' affirming that a full connection can be established. That is, it exploits social convention where you both agree to do something.

Hint
Think outside of the box. Actions can be captured by typing, by sensors, and by any input/output mechanisms on your mobile device (accelerometer, strobe light, screen, touch, microphone, camera, etc.).

Credit to others
This exercise and some of the solutions were inspired by Ken Hinkley's paper listed in the references section, as well as the Bump! app produced by Bump Technologies.

2 Generate at least 10 competing (very different) design concepts.
Before reading on, try it yourself. If you are unsure, take a look at one or two concepts below to get into the right mood, and then continue on your own.

A variety of quickly sketched concepts I came up with are illustrated below. Note that while the sketches are quite simple and crude, they suffice to capture the basic concept. Also note that there is no attempt here to differentiate between good and bad ideas – we are still at the brainstorming stage!

a Entering an agreed upon keyword.
Both people start an 'authentication' program, which merely asks them to type in a word. They decide on a word, and type it in. Because the word matches on both phones, the connection is authenticated.

Both people type a word chosen by them

b Mimicking a rotation pattern.
A person rotates the phone in a certain pattern. The other person watches and does the same pattern within a certain amount of time. The accelerometer data on both phones are checked; if they are similar, the connection is authenticated.

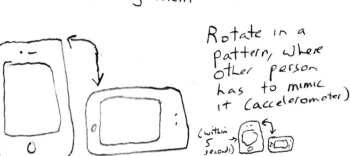

Rotate in a pattern, where other person has to mimic it (accelerometer)

(within 5 seconds)

c Tracing across displays.
The two phones are held side by side and a line appears on the same place on each. One person uses a finger to draw the line across both displays as a single stroke. The touch screens on the phones capture and analyze the timing of the stroke and use that to authenticate the connection.

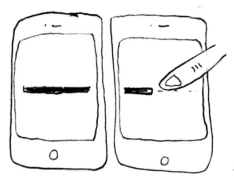

Synchronous gesture
Trace a line across both side by side devices as a single stroke

d Speak a command.
Two phones are held side by side and the word 'connect' is spoken into their microphones. The word is recognized and the volume levels are checked across both phones; if they are similar, the connection is authenticated.

Connect

Microphones pick up spoken command at similar volume

Recognize a phone's flash strobe pattern.
The flash on one phone is turned on as a strobe pattern. The other phone's camera is pointed directly at it. The intensity is checked to make sure that the other phone is very close to the camera, and then the pattern is detected and analyzed to see if it matches.

LED strobe pattern captured by camera

Bump two phones together.
The accelerometer data is compared to see if the same bump pattern occurs at the same time.

Credit: this concept is realized by the Bump Technologies App for the iPhone and the Android.

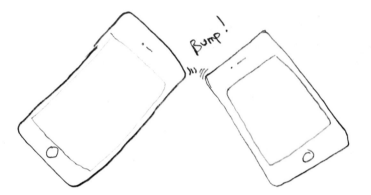

Bump!

Bump. Accelerometer matches bump vibrations

Musical Sequence.
A musical sequence is played on one phone at low volume so it can only be heard by another phone held very close to it. As with other examples, the patterns are compared across phones and if they match, the connection is established.

Faint musical sound played on one device picked up by the other device

h Light / dark patterns.

Some phones are equipped with light sensors. The idea is to touch the surface of two phones directly together in a random back and forth pattern. Because light sensors on both are simultaneously covered, the phones can look for matches in their light/dark patterns and connect them when that match occurs.

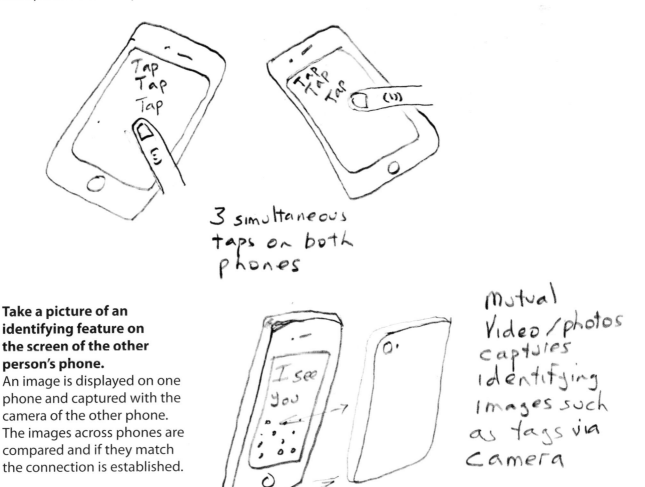

Ambient light sensor Touch surfaces together in a pattern; Both detect same light/dark pattern

i Three simultaneous taps.

Each person has to tap his or her touch screens three times at the same time.

Tap Tap Tap

Tap Tap Tap

3 simultaneous taps on both phones

j Take a picture of an identifying feature on the screen of the other person's phone.

An image is displayed on one phone and captured with the camera of the other phone. The images across phones are compared and if they match the connection is established.

I see you

Mutual video/photos captures identifying images such as tags via camera

Reduce the number of design concepts / Repeat the above as needed.
While there are many approaches above, two themes emerge: a) both people perform an action as a pattern (either in tandem or sequentially) that can be compared, or b) an action begins on one phone and continues on another. At this point, you can generate other possibilities based on these two themes, or try to come up with yet another theme. We won't do this here, but you can try it on your own.

 Choose the most promising design concept as a starting point.
Because cameras are common on almost all smart phones, we decided to explore that concept further by considering variations of how a camera could be used. I chose the concept in the last sketch (J) above, where one person takes a picture of an identifying feature on the other person's phone.

 Produce 10 details and/or variations of a particular design concept.
Try this yourself before you read on. The first sketch below is a detail describing the sequence of steps people would have to do to realize the concept in that last sketch (J) above. The other sketches are alternate ways a camera could be used.

 Detail: What two people would have to do to connect to each other via taking pictures.

    i)   Both have to start the Connect! application on the phone, which gives instructions and displays a unique image.

Both Start Connect! App

SALLY

FRED

Connect!

One of you take a picture of the other's screen

Connect!

One of you take a picture of the other's screen

start up dialog

ii)   One person takes a picture of the other's screen, which captures the unique image that the phone can translate as an identifier. Under the covers, that phone checks to see which nearby phones have that matching ID.

One person takes picture of the other's screen

iii)   Once the connection is established, both people can then choose what they want to share (need to work out the details of this).

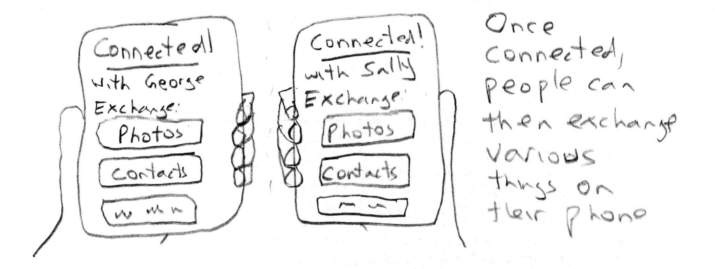

Once connected, people can then exchange various things on their phone

Alternatives: Other ways of using the camera

b

Flashing patterns.
Instead of using a strobe, each screen can generate a sequence of patterns on its display, where it alternates between black and white. If the cameras and screen face each other, then that sequence can be recognized.

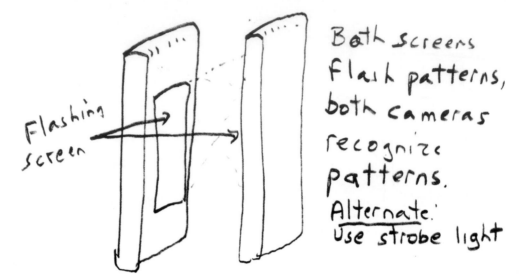

Flashing screen

Both screens flash patterns, both cameras recognize patterns.

Alternate: Use strobe light

c

Fiduciary tag recognition.
Fiduciary tags are an increasingly common way to uniquely identify items. Here, we envisage that every Smart Phone will contain an embedded tag in its case. If the other phone takes a picture of it (which requires it to be very close), a connection is established.

Variation
For added security, both phones would have to take a picture of each other's tags.

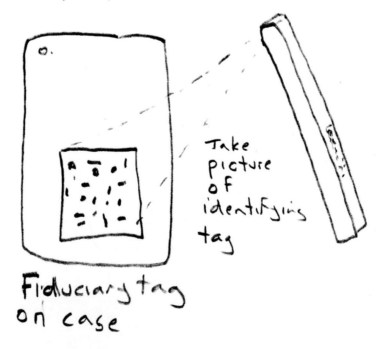

Take picture of identifying tag

Fiduciary tag on case

d **The cooperative panorama.**
Panorama pictures are usually created by a person taking an image, where the camera then displays part of this image on the screen so the person can overlap it correctly to take the next image in the sequence. The cooperative panorama simply does this across the phones: both people take turns taking the next image in the sequence.

Mutual panorama, Person 1 starts a panorama, Person 2 continues it, Person 3 completes it.

e **Take a picture of the same thing at the same time.**
Images are taken of exactly the same thing at the same time at approximately the same position. Images and timing information are compared across phones to see if a match occurs. Note: may fail at crowded tourist sites.

Take picture of the same thing at the same time.

f–j

You try.
We stopped here, as we could fill this book with much more than 5 alternatives, and eventually to designs and redesigns as we progressed down the design funnel.

If you want to continue, a good exercise is to choose one of the above (it doesn't really matter which one), and envisage the progressions of actions that a person would have to do and what the smart phone would show. You would begin at the very beginning (e.g., two people in a room wishing to establish a connection) until the very end (where a connection was established and you could actually start exchanging information). You may find that an idea that seems ok in a single sketch actually doesn't work out well when considered in detail, as it doesn't fit smoothly into an interaction sequence.

6 & 7

Present your best idea(s) to a group and get feedback about it, and then continue to refine and sketch out your idea(s) as your concept changes and as details get worked out.

DESIGN CHALLENGE 2

Imagine you have a pressure-sensitive keyboard, where each key reports the character typed, and its press force, ie., how hard a person was pressing the key. What could you do with this keyboard? Create 10 different ideas of what you could do (it could be something useful or playful), and then choose one or two and create 10 variations of that idea and/or refinements of that idea.

This design challenge was actually proposed as part of the ACM UIST Conference Student Innovation Contest (see http://www.acm.org/uist/uist2009/call/contest.html), where Microsoft provided prototypes of the hardware to contestants. The goal of that contest was to develop new interactions on unique hardware produced by a company.

Want to see what the winners did? Go to these web sites describing each winner's entry as well as other possibilities.
http://www.acm.org/uist/uist2009/program/sicwinners.html and
http://www.youtube.com/watch?v=PDI8eYIASf0 .

DESIGN CHALLENGE 3

Most computer displays have a power save mode. Typically, a person can enter that mode through some manual action (e.g., a menu selection), or the system may do this automatically after a predetermined amount of time. The computer then 'wakes up' when a person moves the mouse. The problem is that if the time-out period is long, screens stay on unnecessarily even when a person is away. While people can switch it off manually, they often don't bother.

Generate alternate approaches to this strategy. If you get stuck, feel free to equip your display (or your environment) with sensors. You will find one solution to this problem in the paper by Greenberg, Marquardt, Ballendat et. al. (2011), listed below.

References

Greenberg, S., Marquardt, N., Ballendat, T., Diaz-Marino, R., and Wang, M. (2011) *Proxemic Interactions: The New Ubicomp?* ACM Interactions, 18(1):42-50. ACM, January-February. http://doi.acm.org/10.1145/1897239.1897250.

Hinkley, K. (2003) *Synchronous gestures for multiple persons and computers.* Proceedings of the 16th annual ACM Symposium on User Interface Software and Technology (UIST'03), ACM Press. http://doi.acm.org/10.1145/964696.964713.

YOU NOW KNOW

The 10 plus 10 strategy is an exercise to help you get started down the design funnel. It is important to try it, not just read about it. If you do it often enough, it will become a habit. Do it on your work projects, and on any interaction design problem you see.

The next time you become frustrated at something on your computer (which will likely be the next time you use a computer), try to restate that problem as a design challenge. Then apply 10 plus 10 to generate solutions and refinements to that problem.

Section 2

Sampling the Real World

While most people think of sketching as a way to generate new ideas, a large part of sketching is about rapidly collecting existing ideas. There is huge value in gathering and sampling material from the world around us. When you capture ideas of others, you can then use those ideas as a starting point: to inspire you into alternate directions, to seed brainstorming, to evolve existing ideas into new ones, to remix a multitude of ideas. You don't have to do this alone: there are ways to preserve these captured ideas so you can share and discuss them with your colleagues.

2.1 **Scribble Sketching** is a way to rapidly capture ideas sparked from what happens in your everyday life

2.2 **Sampling with Cameras** lets you capture visual ideas from the real world as you come across them

2.3 **Collecting Images and Clippings** shows how you can capture, store, organize, and later review ideas inspired by photos, magazine cutouts, web pages, and other found objects

2.4 **Toyboxes and Physical Collections** describes the value of collecting, storing and curating physical artifacts

2.5 **Sharing Found Objects** describes how you can share your collections with your colleagues while still maintaining a level of privacy

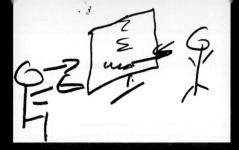
You are in a meeting, and the conversation sparks an idea you think is worth capturing. Or you are trying out an application, and you see an interaction element in it that is worth remembering. Or you are in a movie theatre watching a movie, and you see a futuristic depiction of computers that you want to consider later. In all cases, you are in the middle of other things, so you only have a few moments to capture these ideas in your sketchbook.

This is where **scribble sketching** comes in. Scribbling is all about drawing very quickly, without much attention to detail, and at very low fidelity. Scribble sketching is the same, with the exception that the scribble focuses on the essence of whatever idea you want to capture, sacrificing all other detail. Scribble sketching is an important skill to acquire, and you can acquire it easily just by doing lots of it. This exercise will get you started.

CAPTURING IDEAS IN EXISTING SYSTEMS

In the following examples, you'll do several time-limited scribble sketches (30 seconds each), where your goal is to capture an essential idea shown in these interfaces.

1 Look at the screen shot below (a view of Microsoft's Explorer window for file browsing). Create a scribble sketch that captures a primary idea (for example, the structural layout of the window) as laid out in this view. Use a watch to limit yourself to 30 seconds.

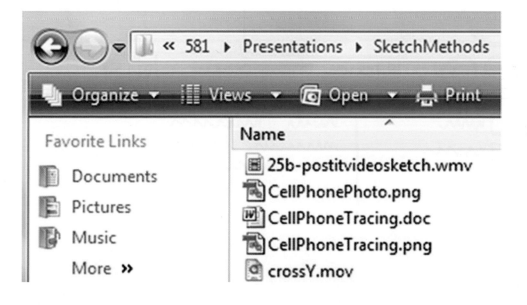

Materials

- pencil

- sketchbook

- a watch that counts in seconds

2 Here is one scribble sketch solution that emphasizes the overall layout into panes and what is in them. Of importance is:

– **What details are included.** Details included highlight the primary concept being captured, in this case, the structure of the panes, and a few key buttons and fields in a stylized form.

– **What is abstracted as a caricature.** Less important aspects are muted somewhat. In this case, the icons and labels (which represent files, folders, and commands) are shown throughout as a box with scribble text.

– **What is left out.** Non-important details are omitted entirely. In this case, all the decorations, actual text and lesser interface controls are excluded. Decorations that make this look good are not included, as are the actual text of the various components.

3 Of course, the scribble sketch you create depends totally on what you want to emphasize. Here is another scribble sketch, also done in about 30 seconds. This sketch captures a different idea, in this case the various interaction methods used in the title bar to rapidly navigate to other folders. Note that this sketch also includes a few annotations to explain the scribbles.

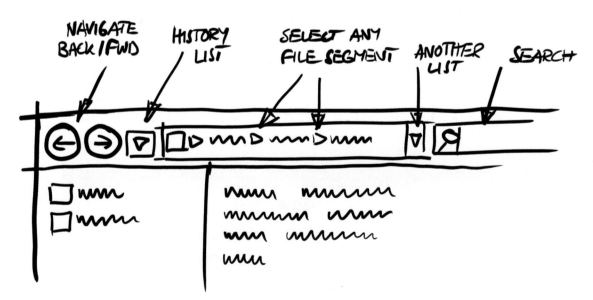

SCRIBBLE SKETCHING IN THE DARK, WHILE DOING OTHER THINGS

The beauty of scribble sketching is that it can be done anywhere, anytime, as long as you have a pencil and something to draw on (preferably a sketchbook so you don't lose it).

Ideas can come from many places, at unusual times. The example below is a scribble sketch I created while watching the movie **Avatar** at the theatre, where it was showing a futuristic control room. The idea that grabbed me was how the monitors were two-sided, i.e., where the image displayed on the screen was visible from its front and back sides. I thought this enhanced screen visibility was an interesting way to provide others with awareness of one's activities, so I scribbled a sketch showing this, as seen below.

I did this while watching the movie, in the dark, without even looking down. I had my first glimpse of the sketch sometime later. Sure, it is crude, and many of the lines are in the wrong spots (although it is surprising how reasonable it turned out). But that didn't matter; the scribble sketch was enough to remind me of the idea: the screen contents visible on both sides, the person using the screen on the left, the walker-by on the right, and both being able to see the screen contents as indicated by the two arrows.

A scribble sketch doesn't have to be beautiful or even meaningful to others. It just needs to capture the idea in a form sufficient to remind the creator (you) of what it is. You can always redraw it later if you want to.

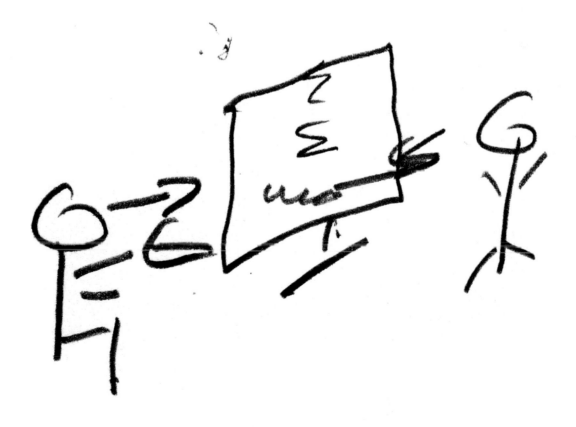

PRACTICING SCRIBBLE SKETCHING

Practice and repetition helps you develop a 'critical eye', where you pull out the essential idea from what you are thinking of or from what you are seeing. Repetition will also help you develop scribble sketching as a habit.

Method 1

Open up an application of your choice on your computer. Giving yourself 30 seconds or less, try to capture the essence of an idea as a scribble sketch. Then repeat this, where you create new scribble sketches that capture different ideas in an application. Now try this again with different – perhaps unfamiliar – applications.

Method 2

Search YouTube or other sites for videos of innovative interfaces. As you are watching them, scribble sketch as many ideas that capture your interest without pausing the video. This will force you to sketch very quickly, i.e., as soon as you see an idea.

Method 3

Redo Method 2, but this time don't look at your drawing while you are sketching. The trick is not to move your hand around that much while scribbling, otherwise your lines will not be in the right place. It takes a bit of practice, but you will be surprised how recognizable things are, at least to you.

YOU NOW KNOW

Scribble sketches:

- are done very rapidly (often in a few seconds),
- serve as a means to capture a critical idea on the fly,
- sacrifice detail and fidelity to speed,
- with practice, can be drawn without looking.

The world is a rich environment – full of factors that you interact with on a daily basis. Some of these may inspire you. Some of these may irritate you. Either way, this is useful information that can feed into current and future design ideas. We've already shown you how a quick scribble sketch is one way for you to capture your impressions of things that spark design thoughts. Another method is by sampling with cameras, where you can capture these moments with a quick picture or two or even as a video. And you can be spontaneous about it if you keep your camera handy with you.

Sampling the real world is all about becoming a hunter and gatherer. It is about gathering what you do notice – both the positive and the negative. It is also about hunting. It is about looking for things that interest you, as well as noticing what you notice. As you move through your daily routines, going to work, stopping in a coffee shop, picking something up at the mall, and taking a walk in the park, you are continuously immersed in a kaleidoscope of sights, sounds and activities. Some of these will attract your attention. Maybe it is an action. Maybe it is a color. Maybe it is a shape. Maybe it is an interaction you need to perform. Your attention is piqued. At a moment like this, a camera can be a handy tool. Take a picture of what intrigued you, or even what irritated you.

SAMPLING OBJECTS THAT IRRITATE YOU AND OTHERS

The simplest way to begin sampling is to photograph situations and objects that irritate you.

Why is this? Well, to become a good designer, you need to also become a good design critic. This means you need to be able to find designs that inspire you (and explain why they inspire you), spot designs that are inadequate, and explain why they are inadequate. Finding poor designs means sensitizing yourself to spot design objects that irritate you, and then trying to understand why the design irritates you. If you can spot bad design, you will begin to look at your own work with a critical eye. A good start to acquire this skill is to sample those kinds of irritating situations and objects from the real world.

Materials

- a digital camera of any kind

Tip

If you are in the market for a camera to use for sampling, consider:

– a pocket-sized camera so you will always have it handy, or

– a cell phone with a decent camera built into it, and

– that the camera includes video capabilities to capture events that unfold over time and/or your commentary about what you are seeing

Tip

Photo sampling is all about a quick snap. Mostly, it is simply about keeping a memory trigger for future use.

Sampling is not about composing a beautiful photo. At its minimum, it just needs to provide you with the essence of what caught your attention.

Samples should be relevant to design thinking. It is NOT about taking snap shots of our friends, our family and exciting natural vistas we visit.

Example 1: Elevator Open and Close Buttons

Start with a simple interaction in your day. For instance, you see your friend approaching the elevator you are already in. You reach for the button to hold the door open, but by mistake you hit the wrong button and the door closes quickly. Or sometimes you hit the iconic symbol instead of the button. You realize that you are not alone in these mistakes. You have seen other people hesitate when they reach for the 'open door' button. What is it about these open and close buttons that makes it so easy to hit the wrong one? Take a quick snap shot of the buttons. Take photos of several elevators.

Reflect on the images you captured. You notice that the raised iconic symbol looks like a button; no wonder you keep pressing that instead of the button. You also notice that while the symbols on these buttons seem quite standardized, their meaning isn't clear at a glance. Why do they cause confusion? Perhaps this is because the symbols for open and close doors are quite similar. Perhaps it is because the triangles are easy symbols to flip in one's mind. Or perhaps its because the graphics are a mix of concrete and abstract symbols – the line for the opening, the arrows for the direction. Maybe standardization in itself is not an answer. The symbols need to be clear and readable first.

Hmmm... how do commercial computer applications manage their many icons? Time to examine those as well. And maybe the icons and other symbols you use in your own graphical screen designs also have these problems? Time to check that...

Example 2:
Automatic Door Openers

I was approaching a well-labelled automatic door carrying a box. I thought how true it was that well designed aids – such as motorized door openers – can make everyone's life easier. Then I noticed that there didn't seem to be a switch for the door I needed to enter. So I struggled instead with the two manual latches on the door after juggling the box around. Where was the electonic switch? This doorway is a short hallway with several other fire doors, all of which are automatic. For three of these doors, the switch is within inches of the door itself. For the door in the photo – the one I had to use – the switch was located about ten feet away, quite close to another one of the doors. My first impression was that there was no switch for this door. I only found the correct one after noticing that one of the other doors seemed to have two switches.

Hmmm... how well are my controls located in my GUIs?

Example 3:
Self-Serve Department Store Checkout

Long lines in the department store checkouts convinced me to use the self-serve checkout, even though I anticipated that I would likely have problems using it. On arriving at the checkout, I saw that the store clerks had already identified and repaired several problems, likely after they repeatedly helped others like me work through the checkout process. Their solution: augment the self-serve checkout with signs giving additional directions. The employee's notes and other grass root repairs identify errors that happen so frequently that they had to find a solution to smooth out the transactions.

Hmmm... does my company's help desk track users' problems with our software? Do they offer standard solutions to those problems?

SAMPLING COMPELLING DESIGNS

When photo sampling, take pictures of designs that inspire you. Similar to sensitizing yourself to bad design, you can sensitize yourself to good design or design elements that you can transfer (perhaps in altered form) to your own designs.

Magnetic power cord connector. I took this photo of the power cord connector for my Apple laptop. Note how it doesn't stick out, which saves space in cramped quarters. More importantly, it attaches itself via a magnet. I loved this design. No more trying to line up connectors in the dark, as it just snaps into place when I bring it close. No more seeing my laptop falling off my desk when I trip over the cord, as the cord just detaches from the laptop. Why aren't all connectors done this way?

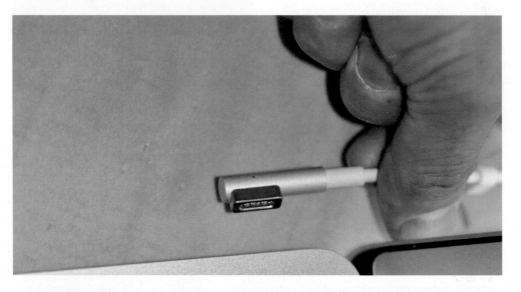

Tips

Make Photo-Sampling a Habit
Take 20 photos a day for the next week that capture designs and situations that irritate you, inspire you, or just pique your interest. You do not have to be sure that the object or situation is truly worthy. This is not about getting a definitive collection. Snap it, save it, and look at it again later.

Make a Found Design Blog
A good way to force yourself to become a hunter-gatherer is to create a blog that shows off photos (or sketches) of your found things. Sift through your collection, and post the ones you find the most interesting to your blog. Add commentary. The act of doing this will make you search and collect objects of interest, and reflect on which of those are worthy of sharing with others. Search the web for terms like "design, interface, found objects, blog" to see how others have done something similar to this. For example, the **Interface Hall of Shame / Hall of Fame** (http://homepage.mac.com/bradster/iarchitect/) collects both good and bad interface designs, along with commentary. While somewhat dated, it illustrates a reflective collection worthy of review by others.

Simplified stitching when taking panorama images. This photo is of me taking panorama images using Microsoft Photosynth on my iPhone.

With other panorama software, I have to manually line up image sequences, which are later stitched together. Photosynth does it all for you on the fly; you just move to the next part of the scene, and it figures out all the alignment. It shows you dynamic previews of stitched shots as you take them. It even draws a green box to tell you that the images are lined up and thus ready to shoot. I concentrate on taking the individual pictures that comprise the panorama, and it does all the other tedious stuff.

Wonderful!

Most visited pages. Google Chrome's web browser lets me use an automatically created 'most visited page' as the first page I see when I open the browser. It's a great way to access one of my frequently visited web sites, which is usually what I want to do when I start my browser. No messing with saving pages as bookmarks. No having to retype URLs for my popular pages. Thumbnails make those pages quickly recognizable. Why isn't there something like this in my PC's file/folder explorer or in Apple's Finder?

3 **Asking a Question of the World**
Alternatively, it is possible to take your camera and ask a question with it. For example, here is a question: how can different shapes be harmoniously packed together? I asked this question of myself in a small strip mall, and took photos of objects that seemed to answer that question in different ways. Here are four of them.

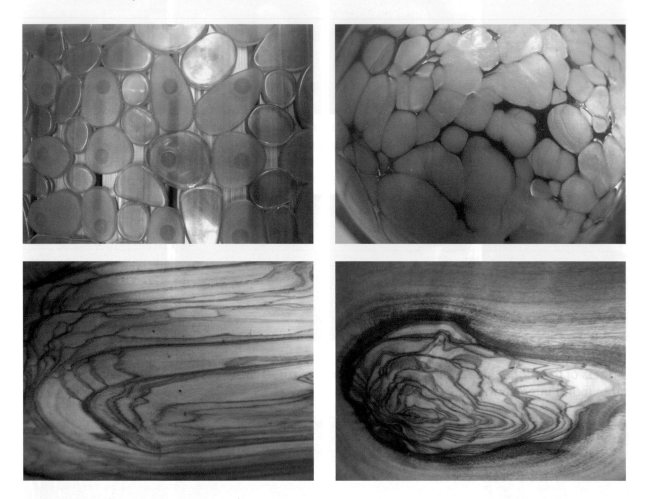

YOU NOW KNOW

1. Photo sampling can provide you with a rich source of ideas.

2. Some of these ideas will hold clues about what to avoid, others will hold possible sources of inspiration.

3. Get into the habit. Photo sampling is a good practice for observing the world around you.

Images now abound – in magazines, in books, in posters, on the web and as part of software. Collecting images and clippings is another way in which you can use the richness of the world around you to fuel your ideation and design processes.

There is almost always a method by which you can save a copy of what you find. You can use scissors to cut out that image in the magazine you just bought. If you can't cut things out, you may use your scanner or camera to capture items in books or posters (see Chapter 2.2). Or you may use image clipping software (also known as screen-grabbing) to capture that interesting interface visual or web image while on a computer.

Once again, part of what you are doing is practicing noticing. Here you collect images that others have created for interfaces, interface design, or visual or digital communication in general. Collect both what you like and what you do not like. Also collect things that others react to, such as when they see something in a way that is quite different from yours. For instance, why did they like this particular interface, which you find close to intolerable?

Remember:

1. Both the positive and the negative are useful.

2. You are a hunter – pay attention to the world around you.

3. You are a gatherer – collecting what you find will enrich your sketch processes.

4. You do not have to be sure – if something made you notice; collect it.

DEVELOPING YOUR COLLECTION

If your growing collection is to be of use to you, you will need to develop habits about how you store your collections. There are three common ways to store collected images.

Materials

For capturing:

- scissors

- scanner

- camera

- image clipping software

- scrap book

For organizing:

- digital archive software

- shoe boxes

- file folders

- sketchbook or scrapbook

1 **On a Computer**
Since most if not all these images will start as digital, a computer may seem like a natural place to store them. However, be careful. A computer is also a place to file things and then forget them. If you do not use, access and annotate your collection you will not be gaining the kind of benefit you could from it.

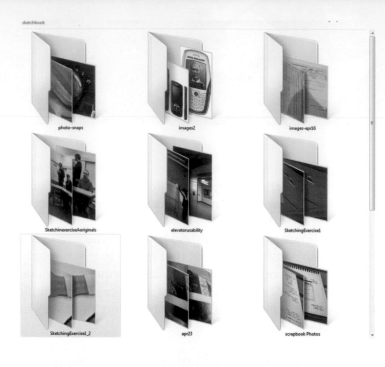

Keeping Digital Archives
You can use digital note taking software – such as *Microsoft OneNote* or *Evernote* – to organize and archive your images and clippings. For example, the screenshot below shows the Evernote archive of one of the authors. Sorting your photos into categories and using tags as keywords makes it easier to find images later (often, with these software tools you can search for keywords or other text in your notes).

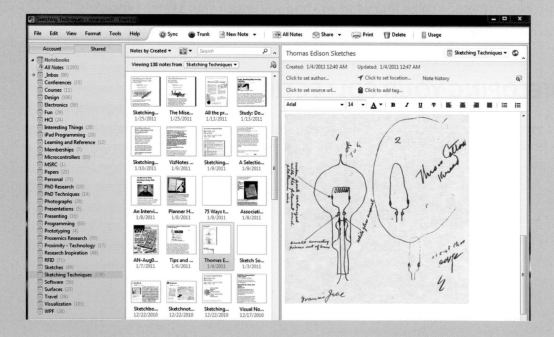

2

In Shoe Boxes or Physical File Folders

Making a printed copy and collecting the images in shoe boxes or physical file folders is another simple way to maintain a loosely organized collection. These are sometimes called *clipping files*. As with the computer file approach, its primary benefit is that it is very quick and easy to get your images into a box or folder. Yet it has a pitfall: accessing may be less quick and easy.

It is through common and frequent access that you will learn from your collection.

3

In a Sketchbook or Scrapbook

You can also collect images in your sketchbook, or you can maintain a separate scrapbook to serve as a visual journal of your found images. In both, you cut out exactly the part of the image that interests you and paste it into your sketchbook or scrapbook. You can add annotations about where you found it along with other explanations and notes. If the image was digitally captured, you can print it out.

We highly recommend this approach for several reasons.

1. The simple act of printing, cutting and pasting often involves a deeper study of the image, including exactly why you would like to look at it again.

2. Any annotation, no matter how seemingly simple at the time, will be very rewarding in the future.

3. Reviewing images is easy, especially if it is part of the sketchbook you carry with you.

In your annotations:

- Include information about where this image came from. Remember that crediting other people's ideas is always important.

- Note which parts you like or dislike.

- Draw and write directly on the images if needed.

- Include any thoughts you may have, such as what things in the image you would find useful, how you would adjust things, or why you would never use such an approach.

Try adding to it daily. if you do, it will become a visual journal. For example, here are sample pages from a sketchbook that also doubles as a type of visual journal. Note the intermixed clippings, sketches, and heavy use of annotations.

EXAMPLES OF COLLECTIONS

Let's take a closer look at some examples of image collections.

This page contains an image showing three colored rectangles atop a photo. The person captured it because it illustrates the idea of layering translucently colored information, where annotations are included within the layers.

In this next page, she applied this annotated layered idea to an interface problem she was working on.

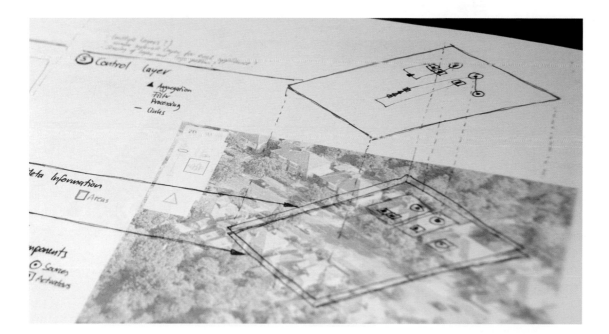

Another page shows two screen shots of data flow visualizations. For this person, these images inspired a new research project.

This page assembles images from the body of related research work relevant for a particular project.

Annotations highlight important aspects of these images.

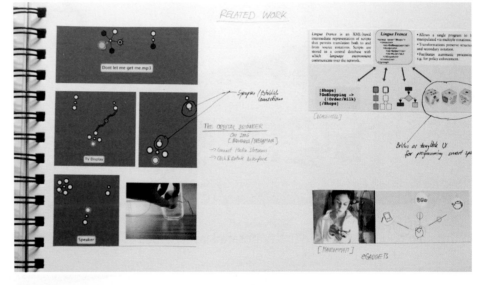

This last page includes scanned images from a book.

While scanning these images ensures high quality reproductions, often it is sufficient (and easier) to take photos of the images with a digital camera and print them later.

References

The following web sites collect images and commentary.

Jacob Nielson's web site on usability: http://www.useit.com/

Jacob Nielsen's AlertBox full of interface bloopers: http://www.useit.com/alertbox/

Jacob Nielsen's list of 10 most common interface mistakes made in movies: http://www.useit.com/alertbox/film-ui-bloopers.html

Information Aesthetics. Where form follows data: http://infosthetics.com/

Visual Complexity: http://www.visualcomplexity.com/vc/

YOU NOW KNOW

1. Hunting and gathering is a continual activity.

2. Any images you encounter in your work and/or leisure activities are of possible interest.

3. Develop your own collection and organization habits.

4. You will know if all this is working if it encourages you to constantly hunt and gather materials, and if you review those materials regularly.

In developing your skills as a hunter and gatherer, you have made scribble sketches, taken photo snapshots, and collected image clippings and scans. This is a great beginning and you will find these practices well worth continuing. However, all of these are images. Our world is 3D, and is full of inspirational physical objects with shape, form and texture. Yes, we recommend you collect physical objects as well. As a hunter-gatherer, you can also collect physical objects to work out new ideas, to re-work previous ones. Make collecting the norm, as it is a cornerstone of an active design practice.

As with images, you can collect and work with physical objects. You can annotate them with labels, show them to others, discuss them, and use them for idea formulation and cross-pollination.

Yet physical objects can provide more than that. Working with collections of existing objects provides a context that can inform and enrich new creations and re-workings of earlier creations. It is like collecting windows into their construction and their history, or like a collection of lessons through which early designers can teach you.

They can be taken apart: deconstructed and reconstructed. Breaking an object into its component parts can teach you about its design process, providing hands-on lessons about the thought processes that led to its construction. Breaking an object into its component parts can also provide you with parts to reassemble in new ways. You can create by re-mixing parts of an object, or parts assembled from many objects.

You can also build things with 3D objects. That is, 3D objects can become part of your sketching process. You can assemble them to make new hybrid objects that demonstrate ideas and concepts.

In this chapter, we will talk about collecting physical objects. We will show you how to develop your own storage and access place where you keep your objects of interest and objects for construction. We will also show you how to curate your collection both for your own use, and for use by others.

Materials

- Boxes, containers, shelves, cabinets and/or other things to hold your physical stuff.

- A place to put it all.

PART ONE: COLLECTING OBJECTS AS IDEA TRIGGERS

The same guidelines apply for collecting physical objects as for collecting images and photos.

1. Collect things that **inspire** you.
2. Collect designs that **interest** you.
3. Collect things that **irritate** you.
4. Collect things that you can **improve**.
5. Collect things that **amuse** you.
6. Collect things **related** to your particular interests, such as existing or historical ways to perform some function.

Do not worry about whether you will use your objects immediately. If they are of interest to you, they may become useful later. Look for old stuff, such as videos, old computers, old devices, old games with odd input devices. Buy the object and experiment with it. To fully appreciate the object, you really need to experience it yourself.

There are many, many places to look for objects. You just have to know how to see them. Pay attention. Observe your surroundings.

1. Look through objects you already have in your house, office, lab, studio, storage, or garage.
2. Go to garage sales.
3. Browse EBay, Craigslist, or similar sites for people to sell old stuff – almost anything ever made is being resold somewhere by someone.
4. Go through dollar stores and hardware stores. You will be surprised what you can find there! Most of the items they sell are cheap.

COLLECTING OBJECTS TO BUILD WITH

So far, we have discussed collecting objects that may help you generate ideas. However, you should also collect objects that can help you construct ideas. The world is far richer than a pencil. A few examples are below.

1 **Collect your favorite kindergarten supplies.** You've spent years learning how to use them. You may as well exploit that.

2 **Collect office supplies. Browse office supply stores and catalogues.** There is a whole industry devoted to constructing things out of paper, sticky notes, transparencies, glue, pens of different thicknesses, and so on. We will show you how to use this in Chapter 3.7: Sketching with Office Supplies.

3 **Collect tools and materials for making physical things.** Keep tools and materials for building your own physical mockups. This may include clay, wood, or foam core (which we show you how to use in Chapter 3.11).

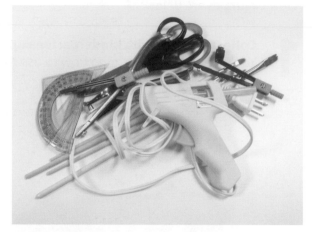

4 **Collect electronic components for making computer-controllable hardware.** Up until a few years ago, prototyping with electronic hardware was limited to electrical engineers and hobbyists. The last decade has changed this considerably.

Lego Mindstorms, for example, is a robot creation environment targeted for children aged 7–16. It provides a variety of sensors and motors that can be attached together and programmed to create robotic toys. We once used it to prototype jewelery worn by distant lovers to caress each other: if one person touched her jewelry, the other (distant) partner would feel it move and could respond accordingly.

For programmers, hardware toolkits such as Phidgets and Arduino let people assemble and construct electronic prototypes in high-level programming languages. Phidgets work as a black box, where a person just plugs in sensors, actuators and switches; no knowledge of electronics is required. While Arduino does require a rudimentary knowledge of electronics (easily acquired by many tutorials found online), it is somewhat more flexible.

5 **Re-use and recycle.**
All kinds of fabulous objects are abandoned. What has become garbage to one process can be a great source of inspiration in design. Textile shops, wood and metal working shops, tiling places, flooring and carpeting stores (and many others) all produce off cuts, remainders, and other left-over materials that are usually discarded. They would be happy to give it to you or sell it for a modest cost.

PART TWO: STORING OBJECTS

Unlike images, 3d objects are bulky, take up space and need somewhere to be. The list below describes alternate storage spaces and containers you may want to consider.

1 **The cardbox box**
Start simple and use a cardboard box. They are readily available, and you can begin collecting right away. However, cardboard boxes are less than ideal. When closed or stacked, you cannot see what is in them. Small items will fall to the bottom and can be hard to find. Larger collections can rapidly lead to a pile of boxes. Also, boxes break down over repeated use.

2 Your desk drawer

You can use your desk drawer. It has many of the same advantages and disadvantages as the cardboard box. The best advantage is that it is immediate – you can start using it right away. It is also probably very close to hand, which is also a benefit. However, it has similar problems in that small items can be hard to find. Space is also more limited.

3 The durable container that reflects your personality

You can improve the quality and appearance of your boxes. Depending on what you choose, they can add an air of elegance to your collection. An example is a child's toybox, or a set of travel trunks.

4 Create a tool cabinet

If you have the space, you can create a display that makes all your objects visible at a glance. One possibility is to create something akin to a tool cabinet. Tool cabinets offer many visibility advantages, but take a lot of organization. They are ideal for displaying a 'permanent' collection of your favorite found objects. Yet because items need to be hung, they work less well for a constantly changing collection of varying objects.

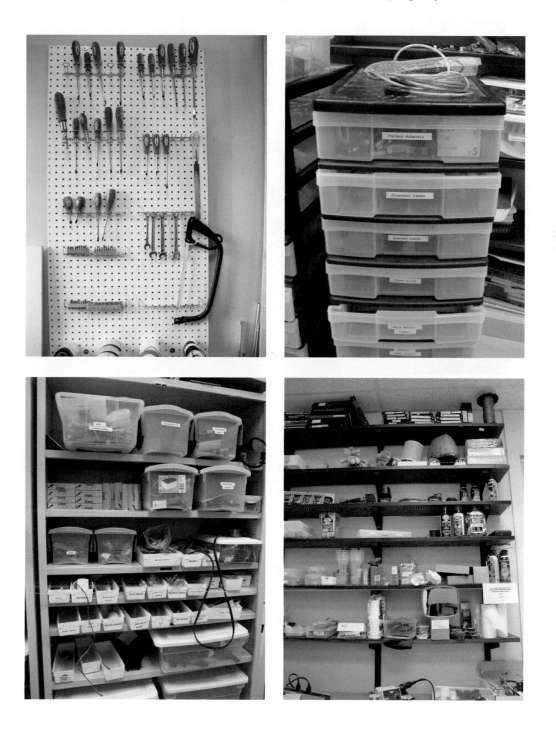

5 **Create a visual display cabinet**
A cabinet with shelving is a wonderful place to keep object collections. Everything is easily accessible. Everything is very visible. Disorganized and semi-organized collections look interesting and intriguing, and can be rifled through. Each shelf can optionally contain different types of objects. It is easy to maintain because by its nature rigid organization is not required. For example, IDEO (a major design firm) uses shelves for its 'Tech Box', illustrated below and on the 1st page, where they can be found at its various world-wide studios.

 Tip
While it is good to think about display cabinets and how you can situate them, don't let that delay you. For now, grab a cardboard box. It will be fabulous because you can start storing your objects right away.

PART THREE: CURATING YOUR OBJECTS

Your collection can be highly personal, where it may contain found items that are only meaningful to you. Part of working with a collection is about looking at the world, and gathering things that may inspire you. However, as your collection grows, it may become more important to organize it for yourself, as well as for sharing it with others.

An organized colleciton is a **curated collection**. You will likely tag and catalog each object with important supplemental information. This is especially true of shared collections, as the viewer may not otherwise have access to critical information supplied by the collector. This is something you are likely to do only for a more permanent collection, as the overhead is high.

One of our favorite examples of a curated collection is by Bill Buxton. whose Buxton Collection collects historical input devices (see References). Originally, Bill collected input and other interactive devices that he found interesting, useful or important in the history of interaction. He stored these in boxes and other nooks and crannies of his house, and used that to inspire much of his writing.

One way of curating is to photograph your objects and organize them as a web site. As your collection grows, you may want to extend your curation efforts to make your objects available to others. The easiest way to do this is to photograph them, and associate any critical information with them. Again, this is something you are likely to do only for a more permanent collection, as the overhead is high. As an example, the images below show snapshots of the Buxton collection of input devices. The first image is the overview page that shows snapshots of all items in his collection, and the ability to filter this collection by the type of input device, the years they were created, the price, the company that created them, and the degrees of freedom.

CASE STUDY: THE BUXTON COLLECTION

The **Buxton Collection** is one of our favorite examples of a personal curated collection (see References). Bill Buxton is somewhat of a pack rat. Bill loved to collect input and other interactive devices he found interesting, useful or important in the history of interaction. He stored these in boxes and other nooks and crannies of his house. He also used his collection to inspire much of his writing on novel input methods, where he always grounded new works in the history of what came before.

Many years later, he decided to transform this into a curated collection. He wanted to bring his collection to a major conference (the ACM CHI Conference in 2011), where large numbers of people could view it. He also wanted to create an easily accessible archive that people could navigate to and view at their leisure. Finally, he wanted this to be a permanent collection, where an outside organization would take it over and display it.

Photo credits: Chuck Needham

He began by creating his own visual display cabinets – shelves – where all items were catalogued by type (e.g., keyboards, touch screens, tablets). He created annotated notes next to every item. Notes included a fiduciary tag, where people access even more information about that item via their cell phone simply by taking a picture of the tag. People could walk around these displays, investigating each device at their leisure. As well, Bill had a running talk to his audience, where he would wander around to different displays and talk about their contents, or respond to an audience member's interest in a particular device.

Bill then crafted a web site to match his physical collection. He photographed his objects, and organized them into an interactive collection. He associated critical information with each item. As an example, the images below show snapshots of the Buxton collection of input devices.

This first image is the overview page that shows snapshots of all items in his collection, and the ability to filter this collection by the type of input device, the years they were created, the price, the company that created them, and the degrees of freedom.

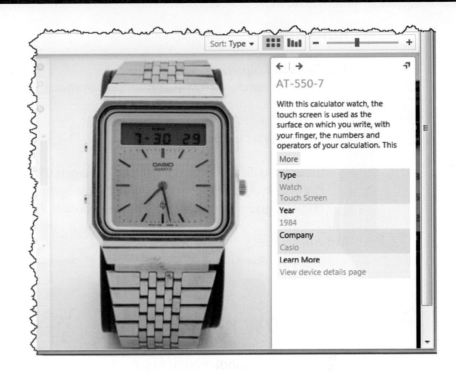

Clicking on a particular item brings up a brief summary of it.

Finally, selecting device details provides additional information. For this touch-sensitive watch, Bill includes advertisements about the watch that he has scanned in, the user's guide that came with the watch, and a video that illustrates him using the touch capabilities of this watch to add numbers together.

What a fantastic resource!

References

The Buxton Collection.
http://research.microsoft.com/en-us/um/people/bibuxton/buxtoncollection/

Phidgets
http://www.phidgets.com

Greenberg, S. and Fitchett, C. (2001) *Phidgets: Easy Development of Physical Interfaces through Physical Widgets.* Proceedings of the ACM Symposium on User Interface Software and Technology – ACM UIST'01. (Orlando, Florida), ACM Press, pages 209–218, November 11–14.

Arduino
http://www.arduino.cc/

YOU NOW KNOW

1. Collecting is fundamental to your design process.
2. Collecting of physical objects helps trigger ideas and discussions.
3. Physical objects can also be deconstructed and/or used as parts of new constructions.
4. How you store and organize your objects can help you and your collaborators learn from them.
5. As your collection grows, active curation can extend its usefulness.

By now you are an active hunter and sampler of the real world. You are a gatherer of scribble sketches, quick photos and snapshots, clipped and scanned images, as well as all sorts of found objects. You should be acquiring quite a collection. You will have sketchbooks, scrapbooks, folders, boxes and even shelves where you keep your sketches, photos, clips and annotated images, and found objects.

Do you wonder about your team workers? What have they collected?

When you view other people's collections, you will find them quite different from yours. You will often be surprised, where you will find their collection delightful and illuminating. Conversations will happen. This is a clear case where you will gain by sharing.

1. Your friends' collections will be new to you and thus new sources of inspiration.
2. Their comments on your own collections will let you see these objects from a fresh point of view.

Of course, it is important to consider your own personal collections from a sharing point of view, as you may have constructed them for different purposes.

For example, a **diary** is an intensely personal record, traditionally of things and thoughts that you do not want other people to see.

Materials

- **your collections of sketches, photos and other found objects**

- **friends and team workers to view your collection**

While **journals** often start as a semi-private document, there is usually an over-arching intention that some or all of it will become public. An example is a scientific notebook that tracks the development of an idea – of intellectual property – over time.

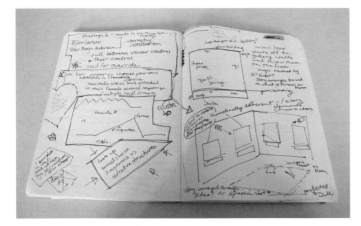

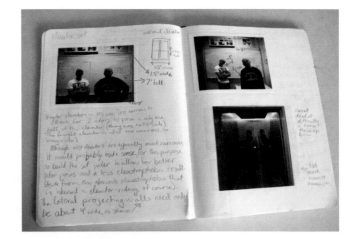

Scrapbooks are commonly built for show and tell. They are showcases made for sharing, usually with close personal colleagues, and often contain embellishments and annotations to better frame or draw someone's attention to particular aspects of the things you've found.

Display cases (Chapter 2.4), **sketchboards** (Chapter 6.4), **web collections** (Chapter 2.4) and several other types of collections are inherently public. They are organized and annotated explicitly to encourage viewing and discussion.

Note

Sometimes things are private.
While this chapter is about the advantages of sharing, we acknowledge that you may want to keep some of your sketches and collections private. That's totally fine. Sometimes fledging ideas can be fragile and sensitive, and you may want some time to incubate that idea before showing it to others. Or perhaps it contains ideas and reactions to other people's design that you may feel are too critical to share. You may want to keep a separate sketching diary for your private ideas, and a more public journal and scrapbook for your more shareable ideas. Whatever practice you follow, it should primarily help you develop a practice and habit of uninhibited sketching and collecting. Sharing particular ideas is a secondary goal, and should not interfere with your primary goal.

MANAGING SHARING/PRIVACY ISSUES AROUND SKETCHING AND COLLECTING

Here are a few simple practical steps to take when sorting out your own balance about private, shared and collaborative sketching and collecting.

1 If you feel the need to be private, start immediately with a sketch or scrap book diary. Do not let hesitations around privacy and perhaps embarrassment stop you from sketching.

Allow yourself to be private while you are learning how to be an active and prolific sketcher and collector.

2 Try starting and maintaining a separated sketch or scrapbook journal that you will share with others. You can do this at the same time as Step 1, or shortly after. Set aside a few minutes a day to decide what can be moved into your journal, and then move them.

This has a couple of positive effects:

- You will start an ongoing dialogue with yourself around what to share and the advantages of sharing.

- When you move a sketch or found object into your shared journal, you may want to re-draw it rather than copy it. You will find the re-drawing process a rich moment of re-thinking, where you will affirm some aspects of your idea and adjust others. Re-drawing or re-sketching is actually a part of most active sketch practices.

YOU NOW KNOW

- Sharing is a great source of idea enrichment so you will want to work toward an active sharing practice.
- Don't let inhibitions about sharing keep you from sketching. Having a dual shared/private practice is fine.
- Re-drawing for sharing has lots of inherent benefits.

Section 3

The Single Image

Your typical sketch will capture a single moment in time, usually as a single scene in your envisioned user experience. While we won't teach you how to be an artist, we will show you a variety of methods you can use to create these sketches.

3.1   **Warm Up to Sketching** is an exercise that takes your pencil for a walk. It serves as your pre-drawing warm up to express yourself and critique others

3.2   **Sketching What You See** is an exercise on drawing what you actually see, instead of what you think you see

3.3   **Sketching Vocabulary** introduces you to the basic building blocks of a sketch that you can create and remix for many different purposes

3.4   **The Vanilla Sketch** reveals the basic elements of a sketch: drawing, annotations, arrow, and notes

3.5   **The Collaborative Sketch** talks about the role of sketching as part of small group design activities

3.6   **Slideware for Drawing** illustrates the powerful capabilities of digital drawing tools, while cautioning about their drawbacks

3.7   **Sketching with Office Supplies** shows you how you can use common office supplies to create designs that are easily altered on the fly

3.8   **Templates** allow you to pre-draw, use, and reuse the constant, non-changeable parts of your sketch

3.9   **Photo Traces** let you create and compile a variety of professional-looking sketch components that are highly reusable

3.10   **Hybrid Sketches** overlays photos with sketches, where sketches add details or emphasize things that could otherwise be missed

3.11   **Sketching with Foam Core** lets you build simple mockups of physical devices by using a few layers of foam core sheets

This simple exercise will help loosen up your approach to sketching, heighten your observational skills and provide a positive place to practice critique skills. This is not a how-to-draw exercise, though it may result in improved drawing skills. This is a practice you can always learn from, which can help keep your sketching skills flexible. You can think of this as a warm up, analogous to stretching before running.

AN EXERCISE IN LINE QUALITY

This exercise is a variation on Paul Klee's discussion around a "drawing is simply a line going for a walk". For this exercise, you need one person to tell a story and one or more people to respond to this story by taking their pencils for a walk. There are two parts to this exercise. Part 1 is about taking your pencil for a walk across your paper: its purpose is to create a line with many variations, rather than a meaningful drawing. The second is about discovering the variation in the line you have drawn, which is a simple exercise in critique.

Part 1: Taking a Pencil for a Walk

1 Gather your paper, pencil and drawing surface – a simple clip board will do. While any pencil will do, a relatively soft pencil (2B, 3B, 4B) is better as it produces lines of different thicknesses more easily.

Materials

- paper
- pencil
- a good flat surface
- a comfortable place to sit
- a story teller
- a story
- at least one person to act as the drawer (several are even better)

2 If you are the person who will be drawing, get into a comfortable position. You should have easy freedom of movement for your drawing hand. Start by putting the tip of your well-sharpened pencil on your paper.

3 If you are the story teller, make sure you know the story you will tell. The story can be made up on the spot as long as you can keep it going smoothly. Or, you can use an existing story, where you read from a printed copy in your hand. I would suggest a children's story with lots of feelings, emotions, and actions without many details. Choose an action-packed emotional story – for instance about losing your paddle when canoeing down rapids, or getting lost in the mountains and coming across a bear.

The story teller starts by checking that all the drawers are ready and announcing that the story is beginning. Speak or read with expression from beginning to end. Approximately 15 minutes of story-telling should be plenty.

The story teller can be free to walk around – this can help keep the story going – but the story teller should make a point of NOT observing the pencils of the drawers as they go for their walks as it may make them feel self-conscious.

4 The drawers start by putting the tip of a well sharpened pencil on their paper and by following these rules.

- Do not lift the pencil off the paper through the whole exercise.

- Do not look at your drawing as you create it.

- The location of the line on the paper does not matter; feel free to wander all over the paper crossing back and over drawing if you feel like it.

- Concentrate on listening to the story and making the line reflect the story, change HOW you are drawing your line as the actions and emotions in the story change.

5 When the story ends, the drawing ends too. At this point you will have one pencil walk sketch per person.

Here are some pencil walks. All differ. They should not be judged, as there are no good or bad sketches – remember that people were not trying to make a drawing.

There are several important benefits from this exercise. Taking a pencil for a walk provides a safe place to practice being spontaneous. You are making a pencil walk, not a drawing.

It also provides a situation in which it is relatively easy to learn about critique. At its best, critique is a process of discovery. Critique is a process of learning to see what it actually presents – instead of what you intended or would like people to see. This exercise lets you experience that discovery.

VARIATIONS

Try different types of pencils, pens, drawing materials.

Try different sizes and types of paper, all qualities of paper can be interesting.

Try creating a setup so that the actual drawing is covered. In this way neither the drawer nor the story teller can see the drawing as it develops.

Try holding your pencil in different ways.

References

Several web sites illustrate variations of this idea. Because you will be repeating this warm-up exercise over time, you may want to try these variations just to mix things up. The following search terms should produce some results.

- Taking your pencil for a walk

- Taking a line for a walk

YOU NOW KNOW

1. A simple line can vary greatly in expression.

2. Drawers' intentions will not necessarily match with viewers' interpretation.

3. Critique is a process of discovery.

4. Critique is about honest observation.

A large part of learning to draw involves learning to reproduce on paper what you are actually seeing. Yet this is difficult for many people. The main challenge is that what registers in our minds as what we are seeing often leaves out or distorts many details of what is actually in the scene. Our thinking mind has many ideas and understandings about what we commonly interact with in our everyday lives. In general these understandings are useful and make our daily activities smoother. However, sometimes these mental models are less than accurate in terms of exactly what is physically present.

For example, quickly look at a person and try to judge where his eyes are in his head. Most people will say they are located within the top third, but the reality is that eyes are almost always in the middle. A drawing based on the idea that the eyes are in the top third of the head would look disturbing.

A good sketcher will draw what she sees rather than what she thinks she sees. Sketching is one activity where strong mental models can be a problem.

AN EXCERCISE IN DRAWING WHAT YOU SEE

In this simple drawing exercise you will learn to draw what you *see* rather than what you *think you see*. Its purpose is to demonstrate the link between drawing what is actually in front of you and creating a good drawing. You will find that carefully drawing what you actually see will rapidly improve your drawings. Betty Edwards, who has taught drawing to non-artists for decades, uses this exercise to introduce drawing skills in her excellent book ***Drawing on the Right Side of the Brain***. She, in particular, suggests copying an upside-down image to help you observe more accurately. We encourage you to get this book, as it is a wonderful primer on drawing.

Materials

- Paper

- Pencil

- A drawing, such as the one included in this chapter.

- A good flat surface to draw upon (a table, a board, an easel)

- A comfortable place to sit (or stand if using an easel)

There are three parts to this exercise. In all of them, you will draw an object familiar to you. Similar to Betty Edwards, we suggest drawing a person, as we all have strong ideas about what a person looks like.

In the first part, you will draw the person from your imagination, i.e., from your 'mind's eye'. In the second part, you will copy a drawing of a person given to you. In the third part, you will flip this drawing upside down, which will force you to copy it as a set of lines. What you should find is a dramatic difference between drawing what is in your head (part 1) *vs.* drawing your mind's interpretation of a drawing (part 2), *vs.* drawing what you actually see (part 3).

PART 1: DRAWING FROM YOUR IMAGINATION

1 Gather your paper, pencil and drawing surface – a simple clip board is handy if you want to move around a bit. It is a good idea to use a relatively soft pencil (2B, 3B, 4B) but any pencil will do.

2 Establish yourself in a comfortable position for drawing with easy freedom of movement for your drawing hand.

3 Draw a person. You see people every day, and you have a well established idea in your mind of what a person looks like. Imaging that person, and simply draw him or her. This may be challenging, but give it a good try.

4 When done, be sure to keep the picture you created. You will need this image after Part II. Here are two drawings made by non-drawers who were given just these simple instructions.

PART 2: COPY A DRAWING OF A PERSON

In this second and third part, you will copy a line drawing of a person. Here you will focus on the lines rather than thinking of this as a person. For starters, use the line drawing below, called **Sean's Afternoon**, by Lindsay MacDonald.

1 As before, get your drawing supplies together and make yourself comfortable.

2 Place the picture of ***Sean's Afternoon*** in front of you. Look at the person in the drawing, then try drawing that person. Copy the drawing, but this time try to copy it as a collection of lines that you see rather than as an image of a person. This is harder than you think, for your mind will constantly see the person, not the lines, which in turn will distort how you draw.

It often helps to be systematic, as you may find it hard to keep track of what you have done vs. what is left to do. Start at one edge and proceed across. Follow the lines with your eyes. Draw each line thinking about its length, how it bends or how it goes straight. Look at how far apart that line is from its surrounding lines, and use that to position it on the page. Draw the lines you see, not legs, bodies, heads, or chairs. Don't label the body parts. Don't try to identify hands or feet. It is just a bunch of lines. When done, keep this picture.

Here are two people's results. Neither of these two people is an artist.

PART 3: DRAWING WHAT YOU ACTUALLY SEE

In this third part, you will copy the same drawing, but this time you will reorient the image you are copying to help you focus on the lines rather than thinking of it as a person. You will find that you can help yourself focus on the lines by orienting the image in a way that the lines do not particularly make much visual sense.

This trick of learning how to focus on the lines by orienting the image upside down, so that the lines do not particularly make much visual sense, has helped many people learn to pay more attention to their own observations while drawing. As Betty Edwards points out, orienting the image differently helps most people look more closely at what they are seeing.

Here is a person copying the image when placed upside down.

1 Place the picture of **Sean's Afternoon** in front of you. **Rotate the image** so it is upside down. This re-orients the image so it appears as merely a collection of lines rather than as a picture of a person. The important criteria is that it should change how you observe the image. Seeing the image as a collection of lines to be drawn one at a time is crucial.

2 Copy the drawing, remembering to copy it as a collection of lines that you see rather than as an image of a person. This may be challenging but in a different way. You will have to ignore your mind's attempt to turn the lines into something recognizable. The best way to do this is to focus on the image details, such as drawing one line at a time. If you have trouble doing this, cover parts of the upside down drawing so you are only seeing the small portion you are currently copying. When you're done, keep this picture as well.

COMPARING THE RESULTS

Take your three pictures from parts I, 2 and 3, place them side-by-side, and examine them. The difference between your mind's eye drawing and the other two of **Sean's Afternoon** is often startling.

Then compare your two drawings of **Sean's Afternoon**. While they will be superficially similar, you will probably find a large improvement in accuracy and detail in your upside-down copy.

Here is a sample of two images created by a non-artist, with part 1 on the left and drawings of **Sean's Afternoon** on the right.

To make help make the differences between part 2 and part 3 clearer, the images on this page are cropped to show a portion of the chair. The improvement is clear, where the second drawing, which was copied from an upside down image, includes much more detail of the chair and has a more natural representation of the form of the elbow.

The point is that this improvement did not come from hours of practice, but from simply changing the way you observe the world.

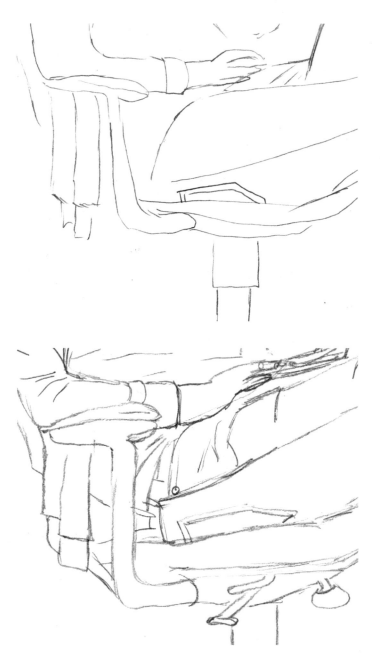

This image was drawn with the source image facing right way up.

This image was drawn with the source image facing upside down.

The same student drew both of these, one immediately after the other. While the first image is recognizable as a person on a chair, the second image, drawn from upside down, is much improved. It still may not exactly match the original but it is much closer.

YOU TRY

Repeat this exercise, not once, but many times. Betty Edwards recommends two excellent drawings that you can use for your next attempts, both readily available on-line by searching for the following terms.

- ***Portrait of Igor Stravinsky*** by Pablo Picasso

- ***A Court Dwarf (c. 1535)*** from the Fogg Art Museum

Make upside drawing a hobby to fill idle time. If you are stuck in a waiting room or on an airplane, look for images to copy in magazines (you will, of course, have your sketchbook and pencil with you: see Chapter 1.3).

Start with line drawing. Then move on to high-contrast photos, i.e., those with sharp edges, where you focus on drawing those edges. Then try to copy things in real life, beginning with simple hard objects (such as a chair), and progressing to softer objects (such as your hand). For hard objects, you will be looking for edges. For softer objects, you will be looking for both edges and for high-contrast features (such as wrinkles and folds in a hand). You can then start experimenting with shading by using the edge of your pencil to darken the blacker parts of what you see.

You will improve hugely with even a modest amount of practice. To illustrate, one of this book's authors (who had not drawn before) had taken a one-day course going through the above exercises. He was asked to draw his hand at the beginning and at the end of the day. His two sketches below show the difference, with the initial drawing on the left and the later drawing on the right. Unlike the first drawing, he concentrated in the second drawing on the lines that form the outline of the hand, the lines that form the wrinkles and tendons in his hand, and the light and dark areas that correspond to the shaded textures of the hand.

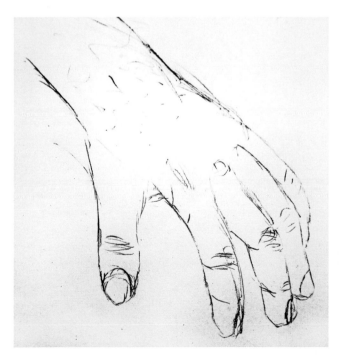

References

Edwards, Betty. *The New Drawing on The Right Side of the Brain*. Penguin Putnam.

YOU NOW KNOW

A large part of drawing is about observing accurately. Observing carefully is something we can all learn but it does take practice.

1. Assumptions about what things should look like can make drawing more difficult.

2. Drawing depends on observation.

3. You can draw better than you thought you could if you stick to direct observation only.

4. Observation and drawing is a skill that you can practice and learn.

Many of your sketches will contain quite similar things – a **sketching vocabulary** of shapes. This sketching vocabulary serves as the basic elements of most sketches. If you practice creating this vocabulary, you will be able to rapidly compose your sketches. This chapter reviews several elements in the basic sketching vocabulary: objects, people, activities, emotions, and posture.

1 Basic Sketch Elements

Lines, rectangles, triangles, and circles will be essential visual elements of many of your sketches. Sketching and drawing tutorials often begin with 'warming up' exercises of filling a page with a random collection of these basic shapes. Become familiar with this variety of shapes. Play with line thickness and hatching styles.

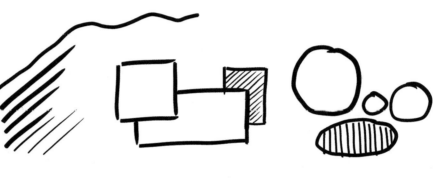

Tip

People Who Sketch on Computers

Libraries of Sketch Elements
Designers sometimes use tablets instead of paper to compose sketches. If this is something you want to do, take advantage of software that lets you save and reuse your sketch elements as a library. For example, and similar to clipart, you can create a variety of elements and save them on a slide in PowerPoint. You can then copy, reuse and maybe even alter them later for use in particular sketches.

Objects
Most drawing software includes a range of drawing primitives: rectangles, circles, arrows, callouts, etc. When choosing software to support your sketching, consider if the range of drawing primitives available suffices to help you in your sketching process.

Clipart
If you use computers for your sketches, you can also take advantage of the many clipart or equivalent libraries of images out there. For example, if you search for 'stick men' on the web, you will likely find many images that fit your purposes.

2 Composing Objects

By combining these basic sketch elements you can compose a variety of shapes and objects that will form part of your sketching vocabulary. Below is a collection of such composed objects – some drawn as simple two dimensional outlines, others in a perspective side view. Remember that simplicity is key: in many sketches it is better to draw objects as simple shapes rather than as detailed and fine grained objects. Note that many of the examples below are in fact very simple combinations of a few rectangles, circles, and lines, but that the level of detail is sufficient to clearly identify the object's function (e.g., the mobile phone, or the photo).

Tools
(pencil, pen, magnifying glass, wrench, scissors)

Digital Devices
(camera, phone, cell phone, computer, mouse)

Documents
(paper, books, photos, piles)

Physical Objects
(tables, chair, boxes, light bulb, clock)

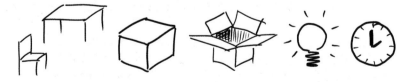

Abstract Shapes
(arrows, signs)

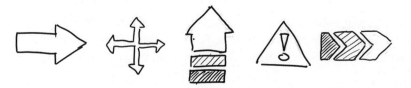

People

Many sketches in interaction design include people performing their actions, motions, and activities while interacting with information technology. There are many different techniques to draw people: from simple stick figures to detailed and realistic outlines of a person. Often, simple stick figures are preferable to detailed drawings of people: they are expressive enough to illustrate people and their actions in a variety of situations.

Alternatively, even comic-like sketches or abstract shapes can represent people in your sketches. The choice of drawing style depends on your preferences, but also on the type of sketch you create. For example, in a drawing that just suggests the presence of people, abstract shapes can be sufficient. But in a sketch of (say) a multi-user tabletop interaction, details about people's postures might be important to portray the interaction techniques.

4 Activities

By varying people's poses you can express a variety of different activities. For example, the sketches below show a person's activities, e.g., running, pointing, lifting a box. Notice how two of the sketches use action lines (also called motion lines) to illustrate the movements of the person's activity (also see Scott McCloud's **Understanding Comics**).

Tips

Learning How to Sketch
This chapter introduces but does not teach you all the different techniques of how to draw. Many books and tutorials are available if you want to improve your drawing skills.

For example, Betty Edward's **Drawing on the Right Side of the Brain** or Kurt Hanks and Larry Belliston's **Rapid Viz** books are excellent primers of drawing and sketching techniques.

Draw a person interacting with a tablet computer in three different situations. For example, you can draw the person while sitting on a chair and reading a book, while showing a document on a tablet to a second person, and while placing the tablet on a table to write a text. Try to vary people's poses and facial expressions.

Our Solution:

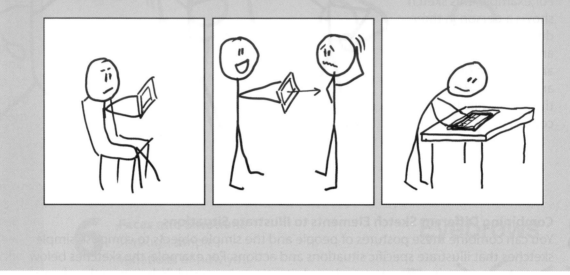

References

Edwards , B. (1999) *The New Drawing on the Right Side of the Brain: A Course in Enhancing Creativity and Artistic Confidence*. Tarcher.

Hanks, K. and Belliston, L. (2006) *Rapid Viz: A New Method for the Rapid Visualization of Ideas*. 3rd Edition, Course Technology PTR.

McCloud, S. (1993) *Understanding Comics. The Invisible Art*. Harper.

McCloud, S. (2006) *Making Comics: Storytelling Secrets of Comics*. Manga and Graphic Novels. Harper.

YOU NOW KNOW

You learned how to build up a sketching vocabulary of simple shapes, objects, and people. By varying postures and facial expressions you can illustrate people in different situations. The sketching vocabulary functions as a starting point for many of your sketches about people's interaction with technology.

But don't stop here! Look for the many primers that teach people how to sketch, especially those oriented toward kids and comic books. As we keep on repeating, you don't have to be a superb artist to sketch. But you will find that knowing and practicing a few of the basics will help you immensely over time.

There are an infinite number of ways you can create a single sketch. However, most simple sketches will comprise the drawing along with optional annotations and notes.

THE DRAWING

The drawing is what most people think of as the result of a sketching activity. For example, the figure below is a sketch of the main screen of an interactive shopping system, expressed solely as a drawing.

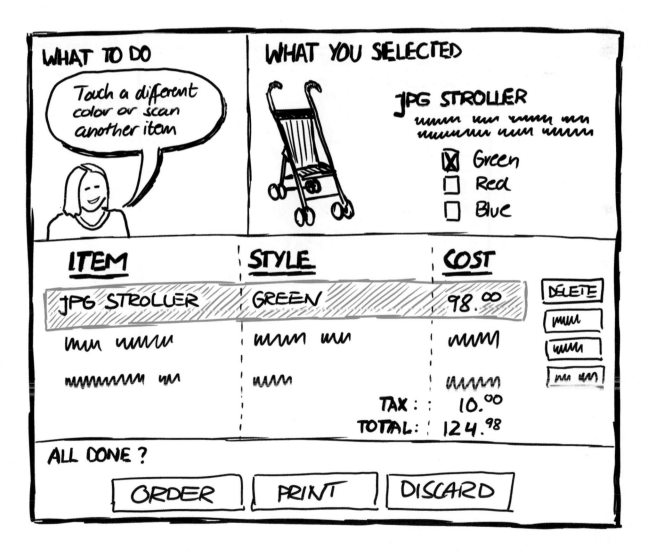

ANNOTATIONS

Annotations are names, labels and explanatory notes whose spatial location identifies the part(s) of the sketch they refer to. That is, annotations are graphical marks that are incorporated into the drawing itself.

Sometimes, their location relative to a part of the drawing is enough to connect the annotation with a particular sketch element. Other times, arrows, lines or braces may clarify that spatial relation. For example, the sketch below now includes annotations. This particular sketch shows various labels and explanatory notes that:

- indicate particular areas of the sketch via braces (e.g., those numbered 1–4 and 7),

- point to specific elements via one or more arrows (numbers 5 and 6),

- are associated by only their spatial placement, such as the label explaining the caricature (number 8),

- indicate dynamics of elements or interactions over time (labeled arrows in the middle of the figure).

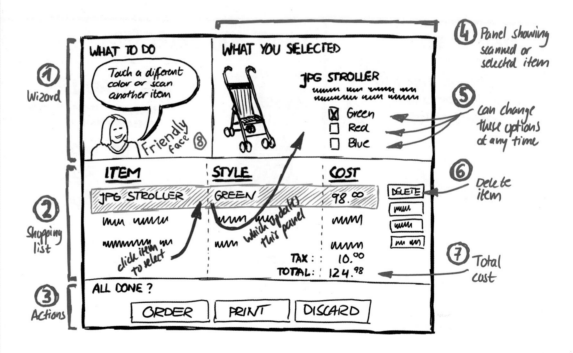

Arrows as Annotations

Arrows deserve special mention as part of an annotation. We already saw in the previous sketch how they can be used to point to one or more areas of the drawing. Arrows can also be used to relate different parts of a drawing, to indicate direction, to show movement, to indicate a sequence of events, to indicate interaction flow.

For example, the set of images on the left below are directions in opening a box, where arrows eloquently indicate the interaction flow and movement (taken from Mijksenaar and Westendorp, 1999). The image on the right is another example, where in this case the person has annotated a photograph of a rock climber to indicate numbered sequences of events, where arrows and labels indicate directions, force, and movement.

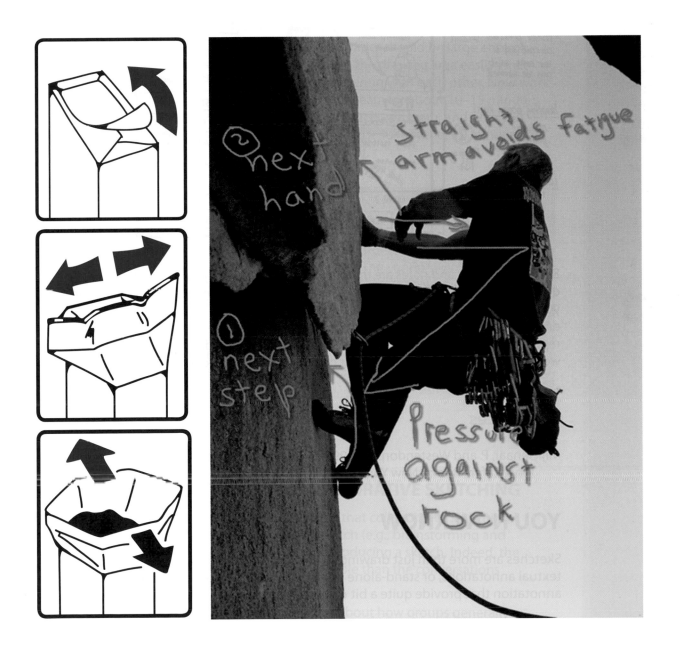

Paper and pen are fantastic sketching tools. They are cheap, portable, and always on. Best yet, you and your colleagues have years of training (since childhood) and experience using a pencil.

However, digital tools have powers that paper and pencil lack. In particular, you can easily modify sketches made with digital drawing tools, make multiple copies, print them repeatedly, use them as templates, and – as we will see in later chapters – create interactive sequences via animations and linking if the tool allows it. As well, if your pencil drawing skills are poor, the digital drawing tool will likely help you produce better looking sketches (if warranted).

In contrast to a paper sketchbook, you will incur some costs when using a digital drawing tool over pen and paper. It will take you time to turn it on, which may inhibit you from capturing ideas on the fly. Unless you have a pen-based computer or equivalent, doing freehand sketching with a mouse is painful. You will have to learn how to use (and remember) the tool's advanced features. You will have to manage your sketches as files rather than as a sequence of pages. You will find it harder to review your sketches, as you now have to find, open, and close these files.

There are many digital drawing tools on the market, and some are even specialized for sketching. In this chapter, we deliberately concentrate on **slideware**, i.e., software used to make slide presentations. We use this software because they have valuable sketching features above and beyond their digital drawing capabilities, and because almost everyone already has one installed on his or her computer and knows how to use it.

SKETCHING IN SLIDEWARE

Software for creating presentations is fairly ubiquitous, with the two most commonly available ones at the time of writing being Microsoft PowerPoint and Apple's Keynote. They have powerful drawing and manipulation tools, as well as access to stock images. We will concentrate on these drawing features in this chapter. In addition, these tools also let you do play sequences as slide shows, and allow for animations and hyperlinking; we will discuss the power of those functions in later chapters.

Materials

- PowerPoint or equivalent slideware system

- a watch for timing yourself

- large sheet of paper, table, and pencils

We will primarily use Microsoft's PowerPoint, illustrated below, as our example slideware tool; other presentation systems are similar. We will just quickly review PowerPoint's basic drawing building blocks, where you draw by creating, moving, copying and manipulating the objects and their properties. You probably know how to do this already. The main point of this chapter, as we will see, is to contrast the powers and weaknesses of using a digital vs. paper-based tool.

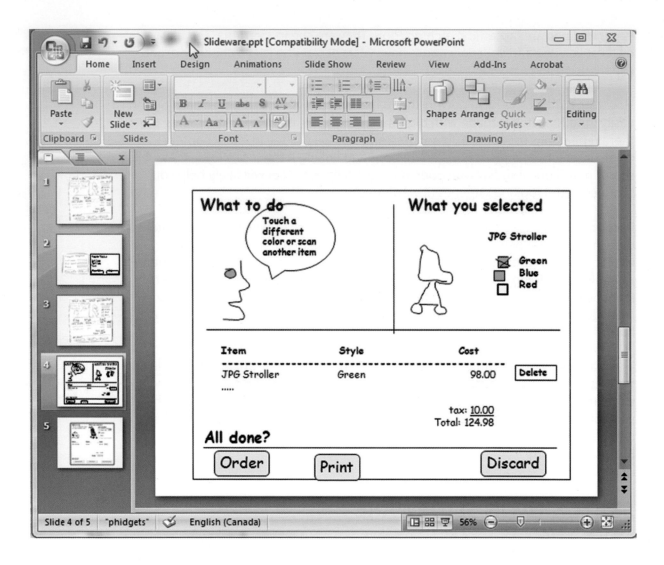

Slideware packages usually have a large variety of pre-defined shapes with many adjustable properties. They also usually include many custom shapes and variations. For example, the PowerPoint **shapes** palette, shown at the right below, illustrates the rich set of pre-defined drawing shapes. The **line** sub-palette included in the shapes palette shows the various types of lines available: straight lines, lines with arrows, lines with corners, curves, splines, and even free-form drawing lines. Properties of already drawn lines can be further altered, for example by changing the thickness (middle figure) and / or switched into one of the many forms of arrows (left), or by changing the color, gradient or even texture (bottom left). **Basic shapes** range from different styles of rectangles, textboxes, circles, different triangles, parallelograms, different kinds of braces, and others. More custom shapes include happy faces, lightning bolts, **flowchart** symbols, various **block arrows**, and **buttons**. There are even various forms of **callouts**, which are excellent for annotating a drawing. Properties of these shapes can be altered at will, e.g., how it is filled or outlined (bottom palette). Of course, presentation packages also include myriad options for text, including font type, size, alignment, color, indentation, character and line spacing, and others (top palettes).

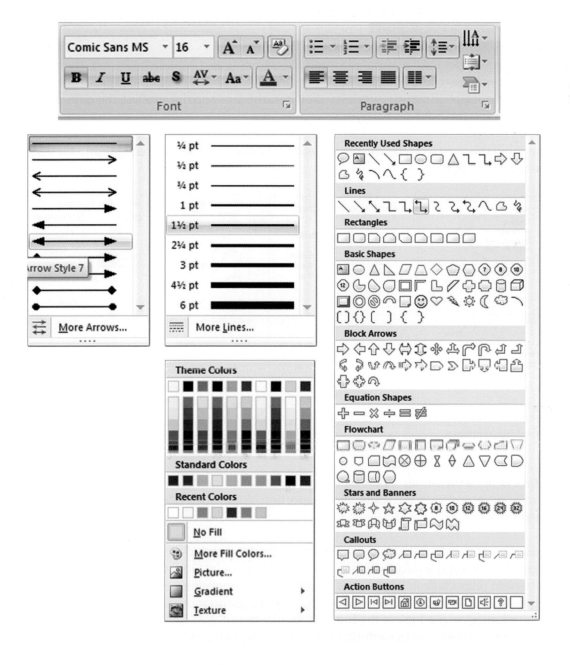

DIGITAL VS PAPER-BASED SKETCHING

To get into the spirit of things, try the following. Time yourself. First, using paper and pencil, quickly reproduce a rough sketch of the shopping system on the right. How long did it take you?

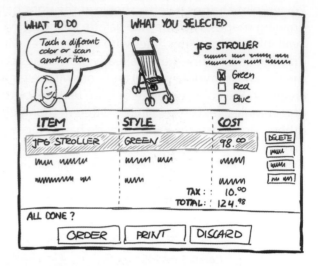

Next, as quickly as possible, try to reconstruct your own version of this same shopping system as a single slide in your own slideware software. How long did that take you?

The version I created, done in PowerPoint, is on the left below. It didn't take that long to do, although it did take me longer than the pencil version. But unlike the pencil sketch, it just looks wrong. This is largely because many of the interface elements are not sketch-like, e.g., their nicely shaped boxes, typed text, and straight lines and corners jar with their sketch-like aspects, including irregular lines, sloppy alignment, low fidelity sketches (the face and the stroller), the differences between sizing, and the poor spatial layout.

Now try redoing the sketch on the left, but instead try to make it look reasonably 'right'. My version is shown below on the right.

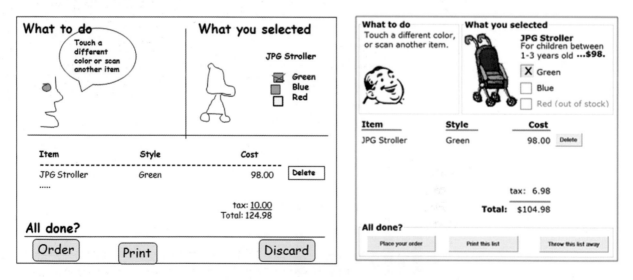

This did take quite a bit longer. I now paid attention to alignment, fonts, color, shading, the placement of graphics, spatial layouts, and proportion. While not perfect, that is why it looks reasonable.

What should be apparent right away is that this 2nd version produces what looks like a high fidelity screen shot. Yet the information contained is more or less identical. While its good looks can be a benefit (especially in later stages of the design funnel), it introduces a problem if done in early stages. To make this 2nd version look good, I had to spend more time deciding on issues such as text size, alignment, the look of the buttons, spatial layout, and so on, which have little to do – and indeed can interfere – with capturing the basic design idea as a quick sketch.

DIGITAL COLLABORATION

Chapter 3.5 already talked about collaborative sketching in detail; for now, what is important to remember is that collaborative sketching on a computer with software is quite different from collaborative sketching with paper and pencil.

Repeat the above exercise, except this time work with another person to (a) create a pencil sketch over a large sheet of paper while seated at a table, and then (b) create the digital sketch while seated in front of a workstation. You will notice that the dynamics will have changed, as in the two figures below that differ only in the sketching technology used. With the computer, one of you may know the software a bit better, and will thus become the 'scribe', perhaps with the other person offering suggestions and directions as you sketch. You may also get in each other's way (especially if three or more people are involved), as seating multiple people in front of the small display becomes crowded. The single mouse and keyboard disallows simultaneous interaction, and forces turn-taking behavior instead (e.g., one person being 'in charge' at a time). You'll also find much of the time is spent choosing and navigating to your interface controls rather than sketching, which will inhibit how you all talk about the sketch as you do it. Participants may also feel somewhat disengaged if the other is doing all the actions.

YOU NOW KNOW

Commonly available slideware applications contain powerful drawing capabilites that allow you to create digital sketches. While going digital provides many powers, it comes at a cost to the look of the sketches you create, the time you spend on them, and how it could inhibit collaborative sketching activities.

While paper and pencil is the best way to create rapid sketches, you can also use other common office supplies to create designs that are easily altered on the fly. The basic idea, advocated in Rettig's 1994 article **Prototyping for Tiny Fingers**, is this. You use sticky notes of various types and sizes as graphical user interface elements, where you assemble these elements onto a poster board to create your layout. You write atop these sticky notes to bring your interface to life. If you change your mind about something, you just peel off that sticky note and replace it with a new one, or move it to a new position to experiment with different layouts. It gives you some of the flexibility of digital tools, while still letting you work with traditional media.

The side bar shows a sampling of office supplies that you will find handy. The most useful are: the sticky notes of various sizes; a sticky-note glue stick that will let you transform any piece of plain, colored or transparent paper into a sticky note; scissors to cut paper and notes into different sizes; and a reasonably stiff and sufficiently large poster board where you can assemble your interface. Of course, there are many other office supplies that you can exploit that aren't included on this list. Visit an office supply store to look for opportunities. Both Marc Rettig and Michael Muller, in their articles listed at the end of this chapter, suggest other places where you can find supplies, or other supplies you can exploit for sketching.

THE VERSATILE STICKY NOTE

Sticky notes come in various sizes. You can also, of course, cut them down to any size. This means you can rapidly use sticky notes as buttons, dialog boxes, menus, icons, tooltips, as individual input fields in a form, as containers of labels and other fixed text, and so on. Samplings of stickies used in this way, along with other office supplies, are shown in the figure to the right.

Materials

- sticky notes of various sizes

- poster boards of various sizes

- 'sticky-note' glue stick

- scissors

- transparencies/ acetate sheets

- sheets of white and colored paper

- water-soluble markers

- pencil

- normal and colored pencils

- sharpener

- good quality eraser

- stapler

- a case to hold these supplies

Try It Yourself

As an exercise, reconstruct one or more pencil sketches that appeared in previous chapters using these (and other) office supplies (try the one shown here of the online shopping system, without looking at my own solution).

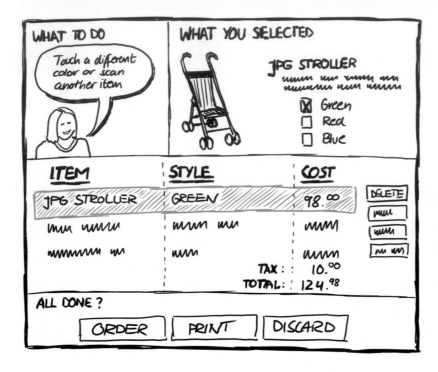

You will quickly discover that you will be making decisions on how much should be put on a single sticky. To help you make these decisions, ask yourself what would serve as the best 'unit' to use as a building block? This will depend on how likely it is that you will be changing the contents or location of a particular graphical element, and how that element matches standard graphical elements of an interface.

Tips

If you know you are going to repeatedly use many graphical elements of a particular type, you can premake sticky notes as that type. For example, let's say you are going to be creating many menus. Instead of doing them one-by-one, you can creat a sheet of menus (like the one on the top right) and make copies of that sheet. You can then cut out these menus, glue them on their backs with sticky note glue, and make your own 'menu pad' (as shown on the bottom right). You can, of course, do the same thing with other graphical items, such as pad of buttons, dialog boxes, and so on. These pads can help speed up your construction of sketches.

The figure below is my reconstruction of the pencil sketch of the online shopping system using office supplies. My decisions regarding sticky note 'units' relate to what I thought I may change as I explore this sketch: the text of the labels, the images used, the contents of the instructions, the item(s) used as examples, the kinds of buttons I wanted, and so on. If you look closely, you will also notice two more 'unusual' things in this sketch. First, one of the sticky notes is of a person's finger, where that finger has selected the first item in the shopping list. Second, the highlight around that first item (invoked when a person selects it) is 'implemented' as a strip of acetate transparency, where an outline was drawn on its edges. I dabbed some sticky note glue onto this transparency, which means I can replace the finger repeatedly atop of the sketch (this is important when the sketch is placed on a wall, so no bits fall off).

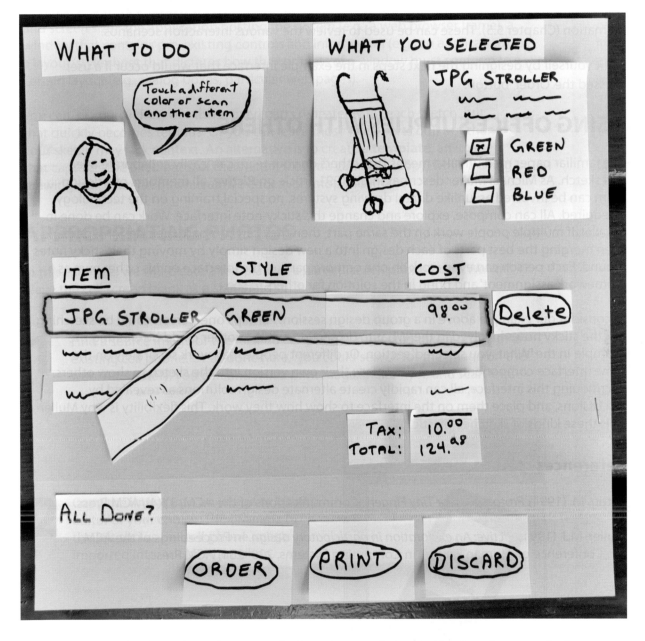

Admittedly, this sketch took me longer to do than the pencil sketch. Yet the advantage is that I can now alter this sketch, For example, I can replace certain sticky notes without having to completely redraw the sketch.

Tips

Mouse vs. Pen: Drawing with a mouse can be difficult. Instead, you may want to consider buying a pen-based tablet; these are much easier to draw with. There is a variety of modestly priced ones on the market.

If you have to use a mouse, zoom into the photo. Its larger size will make tracing easier to do. Still, it's hard to draw long curvy lines accurately. Instead, draw with short strokes, piece by piece. When continuing the stroke, always begin at the end point of the previous stroke so the result is a continuous line.

Drawing in short strokes also means undo will work better when you do make a mistake.

3 White out the screen area, which you will use as your sketching area. In the example on the left, I set Photoshop's paint brush tool to white and painted out the existing screen image.

4 Using your bitmap editor, sketch your ideas atop copies of this image (as done on the left). Alternately, print out paper copies of the images and sketch atop them with pencil.

TRACING

The above technique is simple, but does lead to a perhaps strange juxtaposition of a highly detailed photo and crude sketch. To keep everything at the same sketch fidelity, and perhaps to mute unneeded details, you can create a sketch of the image – the cell phone – and use that as a template. You can do this quickly by **tracing**. Here is one convenient way to do this in software.

1 Load the image into a bitmap editor that lets you create layers. Create a new layer (how you do this depends on your software), and trace over the parts of the image you want to keep. You don't have to trace everything, nor do you need to capture it in full fidelity. In the figure to the right, the letters associated with the keys were left off, and scribble text was used instead of logos.

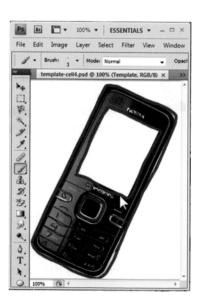

2 Remove, cut or hide the photo layer, leaving only the trace. In Photoshop, you can do this by selecting the layer containing the original image and turning its visibility off, as done below in Layer 1.

3 As before, you can sketch your ideas atop copies of this template.

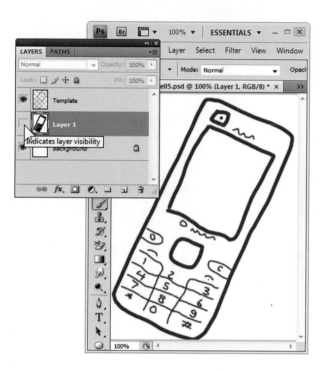

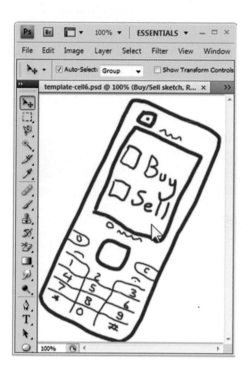

MORE ON LAYERS

Editors that allow layering will let you create and experiment with a multitude of sketches, where each sketch variation is saved as a new layer. This way, you can switch between layers (and between ideas) simply by changing that layer's visibility. You can also build up your single sketch as a series of layers. The examples below show how this is done in Photoshop.

1 Create layers as shown. The first four images show different layers, including the original image (layer titled Cell phone photo), the sketched over template (layer Template), and two different sketches of the screen contents (layers Buy/Sell by cursor, and Buy/Sell by numbers). The visibility of layers was adjusted to hide and reveal particular layers.

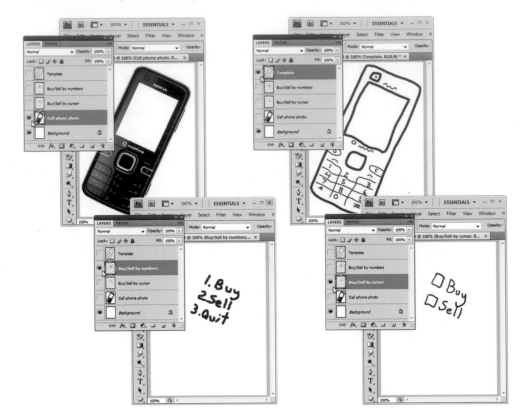

2 Compose the layers together to achieve different sketches. In Photoshop, this is done by adjusting the layer visibility. These images both use two composite layers. Both make the Template layer visible (to show the sketched phone). The first makes the Buy/Sell by numbers layer visible, while the second uses the Buy/Sell by cursor layer. While we don't show this, you can use the phone image instead of the sketched template simply by making the Cell phone photo layer visible and the Template layer invisible.

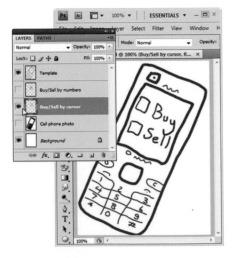

BACK TO PAPER

While software may help you create templates, it is not crucial. And as usual, drawing with pen or pencil is often faster and more convenient than drawing in software.

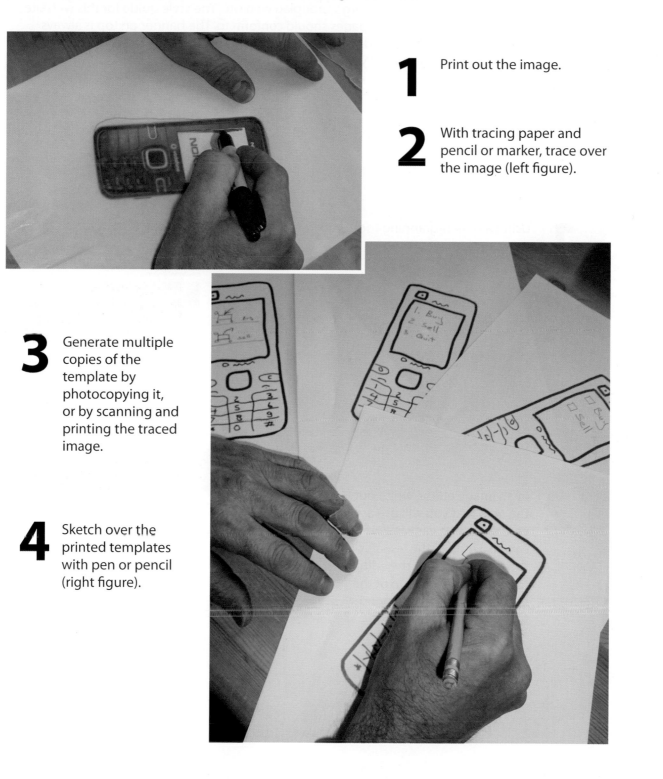

1 Print out the image.

2 With tracing paper and pencil or marker, trace over the image (left figure).

3 Generate multiple copies of the template by photocopying it, or by scanning and printing the traced image.

4 Sketch over the printed templates with pen or pencil (right figure).

ANOTHER EXAMPLE: A WEB PAGE TEMPLATE

The next example shows – in abbreviated form – how the same technique is used to create a template for a web page. In this case, the designer is sketching out the general style of 'Project' pages, a new sub-site within Saul Greenberg's Grouplab web site. The style guide for this web site determined a fixed look and feel that all pages should conform to. The banner on top is always the same (although the highlights may differ), as is the sidebar. These are the steps the designer did, which you can repeat on this site or your own preferred web site.

1 Using a screen-grabbing tool, grab the source image.

2 In an image editor, white out the area that you will use as your sketching canvas. You can also modify the visuals of the template using the editing tools (e.g., the location of the blue highlight was changed to be over the Projects tab).

3 Using that as your template, sketch out your ideas. The two at the bottom are two variations of layout ideas for a project page. In this case, we used the image editor tools to create the layouts.

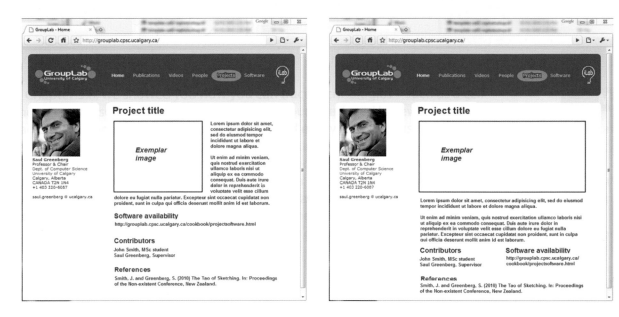

YOU NOW KNOW

Templates are images that capture fixed parts of the system, while leaving white space for your sketched ideas. Templates can be:

- photos,
- traces,
- used in digital or paper form,
- rapidly reused and built upon via layers.

Tips

Photo Perspective:
Select an appropriate perspective for shooting the photographs: from above, at an angle, or from the side. The best perspective will depend on how you want to use your sketch elements. To achieve a consistent collection of sketch elements, we take all the photos from the same perspective view by mounting the camera on a tripod.

Stroke Thickness:
Most drawing systems have a very thin stroke thickness by default (e.g., 1 pixel).

Instead, draw with a thicker stroke. You will find it easier to (a) see your trace, and (b) produce a rough sketch quickly. A thicker stroke will also make your sketch appear more sketchlike, i.e., like a cartoon.

Most editors will let you adjust your stroke thickness afterwards, which will let you fine tune your trace's appearance.

2 Import the first photo of a hand posture into your digital drawing editor. Set the opacity of this photo to 50%, which makes it easier to draw the trace outline. Also, set the stoke thickness to a modestly thick stroke (see Tips sidebar).

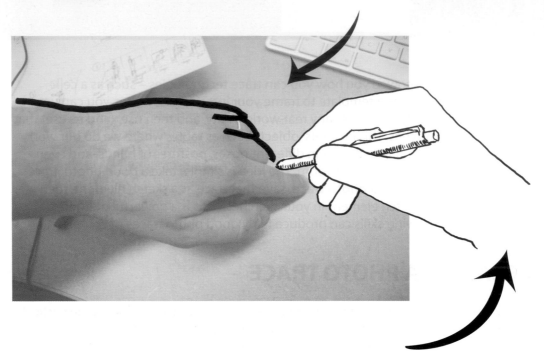

3 Draw a stroke path along the outline of the hand. It is not necessary to be too accurate with this – the idea is to capture the basic shape outline of the hand as can be seen in the picture above.

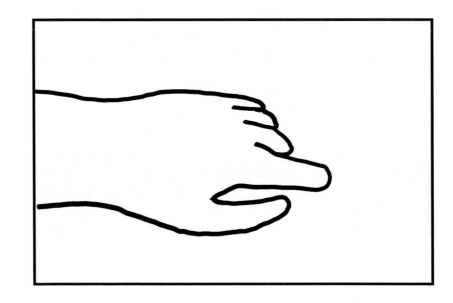

4 Remove the original photo from the background (or hide it if its a layer, as in Chapter 3.8). What remains on the drawing page is the outline of the hand posture that you can fine tune (e.g., to scale, to rotate, to re-adjust stroke thickness) and save for later use.

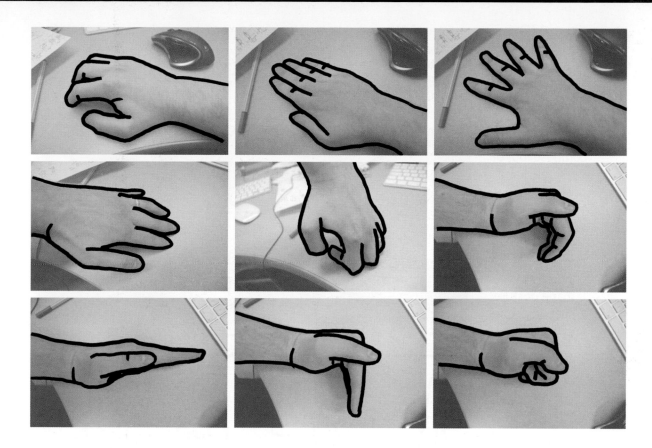

5 Repeat steps 1 to 4 for any other hand postures you would like to add to your collection.

USING THE PHOTO TRACES

Example 1: Sequence of Hand Postures

1 Now imagine that you need to sketch out a particular gesture that a horizontal display – a digital table – will understand. To do this, select the appropriate hand sketches to create a time series that shows a person's hand in different postures over time. Our example uses an open palm forming into a fist.

2 In our solution, we rotate our drawings to present a top-down view of the postures we want. We then compose four of the single hand posture outlines into a single sketch to create a sequence: from straight hand, to an L-shape posture, C-shape posture, and the fist.

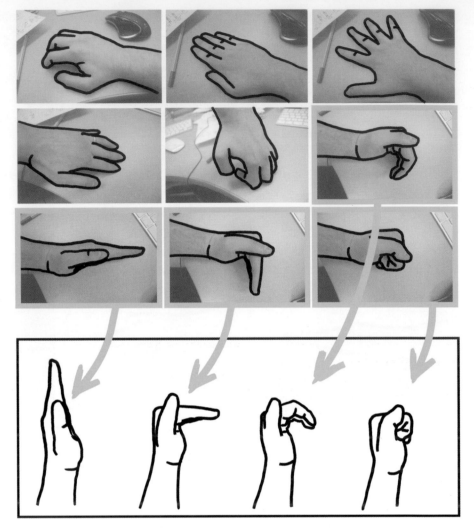

 3 We then add additional parts of the sequence sketch. In this version of our sketch, arrows now indicate how the orientation of parts of the hand relative to one another are tracked to recognize postures on an interactive tabletop, as viewed from above.

Example 2: Using a Single Sketch Element for Two Different Sketches

The two examples below are part of a series of sketches illustrating possible forms of gestural interactions above an interactive tabletop surface, where the surface recognizes objects in the person's hand. We again begin with a simple outline of a hand posture, but here we use only a single hand sketch to illustrate two different situations. The key idea is that we simplified constructing these sketches by reusing that single hand outline and drawing around it.

1 Using photo traces, create an outline of a grabbing/holding posture of a hand. This posture is reused in all sketches in this example.

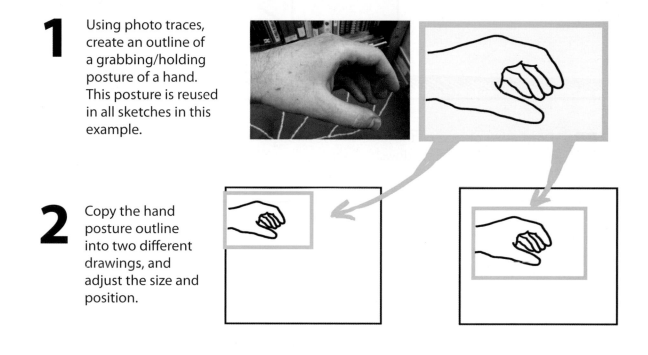

2 Copy the hand posture outline into two different drawings, and adjust the size and position.

3 Sketch the physical objects the hand is holding; e.g., a little cube or box.

Next, sketch parts of the interactive tabletop surface. These are straight lines for the outline of the table, and a cross-hatched shadow at the side of the table.

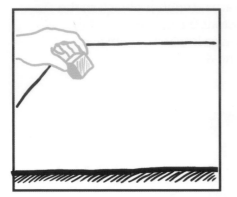

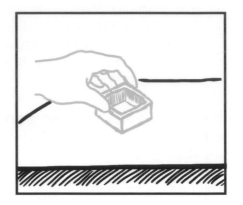

 Draw other objects on the table, or visualizations displayed on the tabletop surface (e.g., virtual shadows).

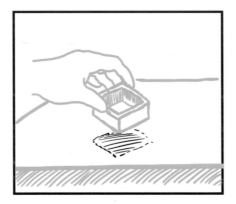

 For the final sketches, add any annotations to the sketch, such as arrows indicating movements and gestures. Using a different color for these annotations can clarify the fact that these are not part of the actual drawing itself, but meta annotations.

7 These two sketches were part of a larger collection of images we had developed to illustrate how a person might interact with digital content on an interactive tabletop by performing gestures above the surface (see Marquardt et. al, 2011). Below are further samples of this collection of sketches; all of them using the photo trace technique as a starting point for generating the outlines of hands. We used the same technique to generate the various devices and objects below, e.g., the cell phone, the tablet, and the transparent acrylic sheet. For practice, try using photo traces to reproduce some of these sketches.

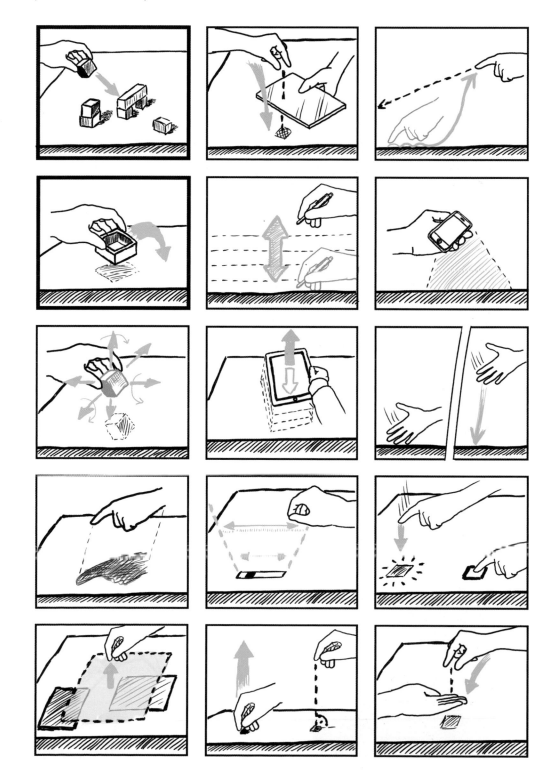

Take a photo of a control panel of any kitchen or household appliance (e.g., microwave, oven). Your challenge is to imagine that this appliance has a touch panel instead of these controls, and that you have to design an interface for that touch panel.

Create a hybrid trace of a touch screen atop the stove. Then sketch at least three different ways that illustrate how you could reproduce the functionality offered by the physical controls. Use a black marker or felt tip pen to increase visibility of the sketched portion of the hybrid sketch.

As a further exercise, stick to the physical controls, where you sketch variations of the layout and design of these physical controls over the existing photo.

References

Greenberg, S., Marquardt, N., Ballendat, T., Diaz-Marino, R., and Wang, M. (2011) *Proxemic Interactions: The New Ubicomp?* ACM Interactions, 18(1):42–50. ACM, January–February.

YOU NOW KNOW

Hybrid sketches have several purposes. They let you add information about the location's context to the sketch. By overlaying photos with sketches, you can emphasize and annotate people's interaction that could otherwise be missed. They can also show how you can vary existing designs by emphasizing what your redesign would add to it.

Most people think of sketching as something done with paper and pen (or digital equivalents). Yet sketching can also be done by creating physical mock-ups of devices and situations. Architects do this when they create scale models of buildings and their surrounds. Industrial designers do this by crafting models of their devices out of clay. Some interaction designers also construct interactive scale models of devices, often using foam core sheets and other everyday materials (such as cardboard) as their medium. Unlike a paper sketch that represents a device, you can have others actually 'operate' your physical device.

In this chapter, you will learn how to build simple mockups of physical devices by using few layers of foam core sheets. You will see that you can use this approach to rebuild and extend low fidelity imitations of existing devices, and to realize a physical design of device that may exist only in your imagination.

METHOD 1: SKETCHING A NOVEL INTERFACE FOR A DIGITAL WATCH

We will introduce you to foam core by having you build a foam core model of a digital armband watch that includes a touch screen interface. The result will be an arm wearing the watch, where one can change what the watch displays by sliding a strip of paper underneath the display that contains a storyboard of the watch's screens (see image at end).

Materials

- foam core sheets, around 5 mm thick (available at most art and larger office supply stores)

- several sheets of paper and pens

- scissors

- cutting knife, e.g., an X-acto or drywall knife

- glue

- photo camera and printer

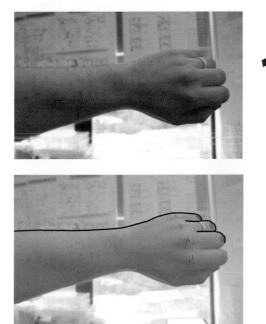

1 Take a photo of a person's arm, and create a photo trace sketch as described in Chapter 3.9.

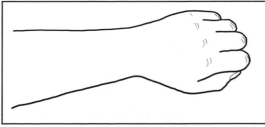

2 Sketch an armband watch over this sketch trace. Make the watch display fairly large, as you will be illustrating screens within it later.

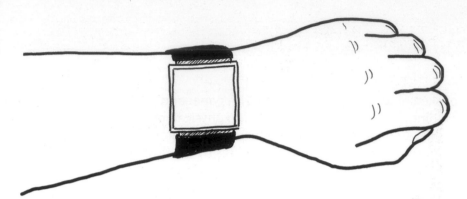

3 Print the sketch at the correct scale, i.e., so that the hand and arm are life-size. You can usually do this by manipulating the scale settings in your application's print settings or your computer's print dialog box.

4 Glue the printed sketch onto one of the foam core sheets.

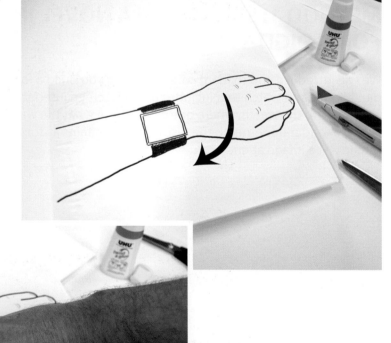

5 Cut out a rectangular area around the sketch.

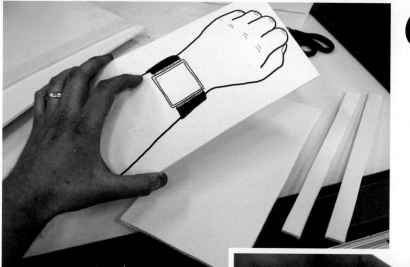

6 Cut a second piece of the foam core sheet so it is the same size as the sheet containing the arm.

Then cut two thinner strips of the same length and set them aside. We will use these shortly to create a 'tray' underneath the arm that holds a storyboard.

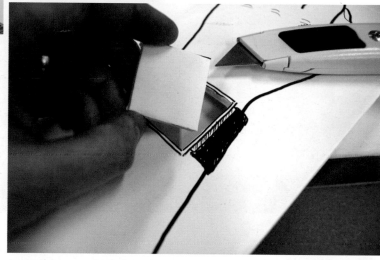

7 Cut out the center area of the display.

8 Create the foam core tray. This will allow you to slide a storyboard under the watch display. First, glue two strips at the sides of the rectangular cut out. Then glue that assembly to the underside of the watch. This will create a hollow channel under the arm.

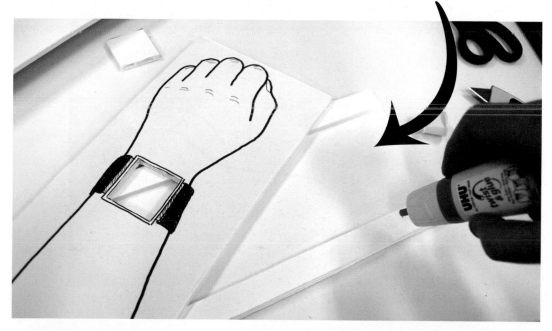

9 The next step is to sketch out a storyboard sequence (Chapter 4.1), where the storyboard displays a sequence of sketches that will appear in the the cut-out square that comprises the watch display. First, cut out long strips of paper the same width as the channel in the foam core model (you can glue several shorter strip together to make a long strip; the longer the strip, the more space for screens in your storyboard). The idea is to slide this piece of paper into the channel, where each storyboard screen will appear under the watch display.

10 Slide this paper strip into the model and use a pencil to draw outlines of the display onto the paper strip. After each drawn rectangle, slide the paper strip further until the just drawn rectangle disappears. Continue until you have a series of rectangles on the paper.

11 Using one or more of the techniques learned in earlier chapters, sketch the storyboard as a series of graphical user interface screens that fit within these boxes. Chapter 4.1 will discuss storyboards in more detail.

12 The foam core and paper prototype of our touch-screen watch is now finished. Demonstrate interaction with the watch to another person by sliding through a sequence of user interface stages on the paper strips. You can even have them 'touch' the appropriate control before moving to the next screen.

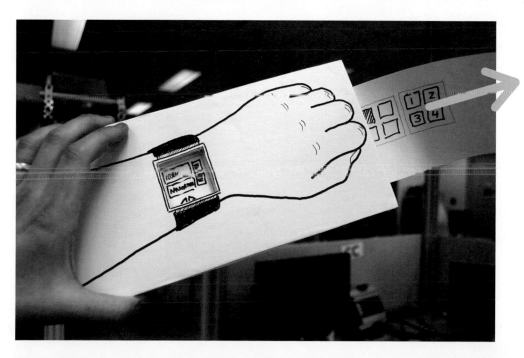

13 Instead of sketching each screen by hand, you can also print out screens created digitally; the only constraint is that the screen size must fit the size of the cut-out. For example, the image below illustrates screens created for a user interface sequence discussed in the next section of this book (Chapters 4.1 – 4.3).

14 As an exercise, create multiple storyboards, each showing a different aspect of the watch, or a different scenario of use, or perhaps even a different way of interacting with the watch. For example, use the same foam core model (but different storyboards) to create a watch that responds to single touch, to multi-touch, and to voice input.

Variation

The foam core model below is a prototype of a hand-held device. Unlike our above example that is mounted on a foam core 'arm', the device is used directly.

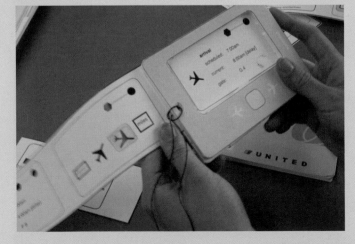

The buttons on the device as well as the sketches were produced digitally, giving the prototype a much more realistic 'final' appearance. This is appropriate for a sketch far down in the design funnel.

The image illustrates a project by Sue-Tze Tan from the Department of Industrial Design, University of Washington, and is reproduced from Bill Buxton's *Sketching The User Experience*.

METHOD 2: USING PHOTOS TO PROTOTYPE EXISTING DEVICES

Many interaction designs involve legacy devices, where the interaction designer has to build an interface that works within the constraints of an existing device, such as a smart phone or a tablet computer. Somewhat similar to the technique shown above, you can build simple mockups of existing devices out of foam core. The idea is to paste photos of such devices atop the foam core. This gives your model a realistic appearance and size (the front layer). As in the previous example, you then create a back and middle layer to hold the screens you design.

1 Begin with a front-facing photo of the device you are interested in. Our example uses a specific mobile phone. If it's a popular device, you will likely find a suitable photo by searching the web. Otherwise, take a photo of its front side, as we did below.

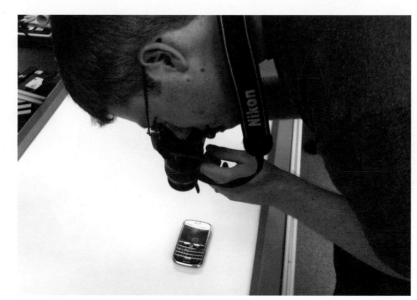

2 Print out the photo of the device. Make sure to use the right printing scale factor to make it life-size.

3 Glue the photo atop one of the foam core sheets.

4 Cut around the phone's outline so only the photo surface is visible.

5 Cut out the opening that you want to use as displays (e.g., the center area of the phone).

6 Create the phone's back and middle layer.
For the back layer, cut some foam core the same size as the front layer.
For the middle layer, cut foam core the same size as the front layer, but also cut into it a U-shaped space that will create a 'foam core sandwich' that holds the displays.

7 Glue the foam core pieces together: back layer, middle layer, and front layer.

8 This particular foam core model only holds one screen at a time. Consequently, create sketches of each screen on small pieces of stiff paper (e.g., cut from index cards), each ordered in a sequence. Cut the sheets of paper in the same width as our opening of the foam core model. Make the height of these cards a little bit longer so that a 1–2 cm part of the paper comes out of the foam core model once we put the sketches inside. This way it is easier to grab each page and slide it out of the device once you go through your interaction sequence later.

9 To demonstrate interaction with this device, put the paper cards with the interface sketches inside the foam core model. Then take out one card after another.

10 To illustrate a sequence, slide the paper into the middle section of the foam core sandwich. Have the 'user' perform an action, then remove that sheet and replace it with the appropriate next screen.

Note

The strips in the first example are convenient and provide a smooth demonstration, as you just have to slide the strip in the tray. However, it is limited to show a strict sequential sequence (see Chapter 4.1). The individual cards in the second example are less convenient to show and display, but are far more flexible. The next screen can be one of several available, where the one chosen and slid into the foam core model depends on the user's action (see branching storyboards, Chapter 4.3). As well, alternate screens can be sketched at any point and slid into the model. For example, a discussion with the user of your prototype may inspire a new screen design, which can be sketched and tried out immediately.

There are many other materials available that can be used to create physical props and models. Some are easily used and formed, such as with clay and wire. Others require special tools, such as wood, but the result will be a more robust and durable model. Still others require specialized equipment and knowledge, such as using 3D printers to create highly detailed and still durable models.

YOU NOW KNOW

You can now create sketches out of physical materials such as foam core sheets. By simply cutting the boards and gluing them together you can quickly create physical props and models imitating the form factor of your end device. Paper-pencil storyboards and sketches can then be used in conjunction with your model to simulate the interaction with that device.

Section 4

Snapshots in Time: The Visual Narrative

What makes interaction design unique is that it imagines a person's behavior as he or she interacts with a system over time. Storyboards capture this element of time as a series of discrete images that visually narrates what is going on scene by scene.

4.1 **Sequential Storyboards** introduces the storyboard as visual narrative that captures key ideas as a sequence of frames unfolding over time

4.2 **The State Transition Diagram** formalizes the storyboard. It represents interaction states, transitions triggered by interactions, and multiple decision paths through the storyboard

4.3 **The Branching Storyboard** reveals the branching storyboard as a way to visually illustrate decision paths that occur over time

4.4 **The Narrative Storyboard** tells a story about the interaction context: the physical environment, the actions of people, and events that unfold over time

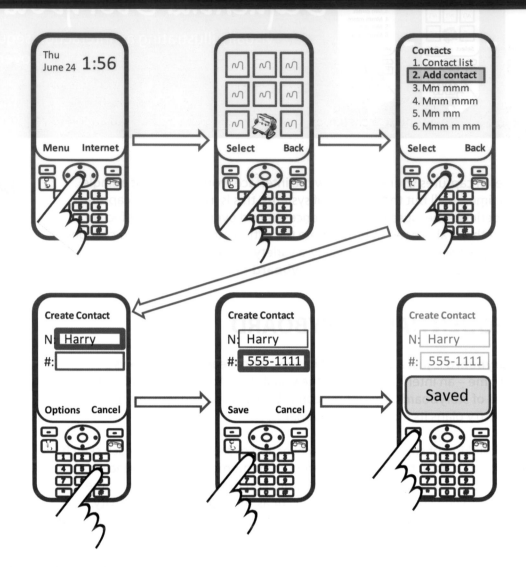

More relevant than how I made these visuals are the decisions I had to make in deciding how the sequence would unfold. Did you find yourself making similar decisions?

- **Should I show the user in the scene?** Is that extra detail worth it? In my storyboard, I decided to include a person's finger, as it shows what was done to initiate transitions between frames.

- **What key frames should I use to create the sequence?** If the storyboard recorded every single action the user took (e.g., every key press) and interface response, it would be excessively long. Instead, I chose key images to capture the essence of the sequence. For example, frames 4 and 5 each represent entering a string of letters for the name and phone number. I decided to leave out the details of how this is done as unnecessary elaboration.

- **What key transitions should I show?** As mentioned, each frame represents a state where the empty space between successive frames includes transitions caused by some user action. You have to decide what transition details are worth showing (perhaps as more fine-grained states and transitions) and what you should leave out. Each transition may actually include many minor user interactions and visuals that are just not worth showing in detail. In the above, I decided to include the transitions that show how one navigates from the home screen (frame 1) to the top-level functions menu (frame 2), to the menu where I can select the 'Add Contact', and so on. However, I left out actually selecting the contact icon in Frame 2, and navigating to the 'Add Contact' menu item, as I thought that could be easily filled in by the viewer's imagination.

Annotating Images and States

When you create a storyboard solely using images, you are leaving it up to the viewer to reconstruct what the individual frames mean, what the empty space between the frames – the transitions – have left out, and (sometimes) what the user did to make all that part of the sequence happen. You already know how to annotate a sketch, and the same thing can be done to annotate your frames as needed. What is more important is that you should also annotate the transitions.

Exercise

Annotate your frames and transitions so that a person unfamiliar with this sequence can easily understand it.

My version is shown below.

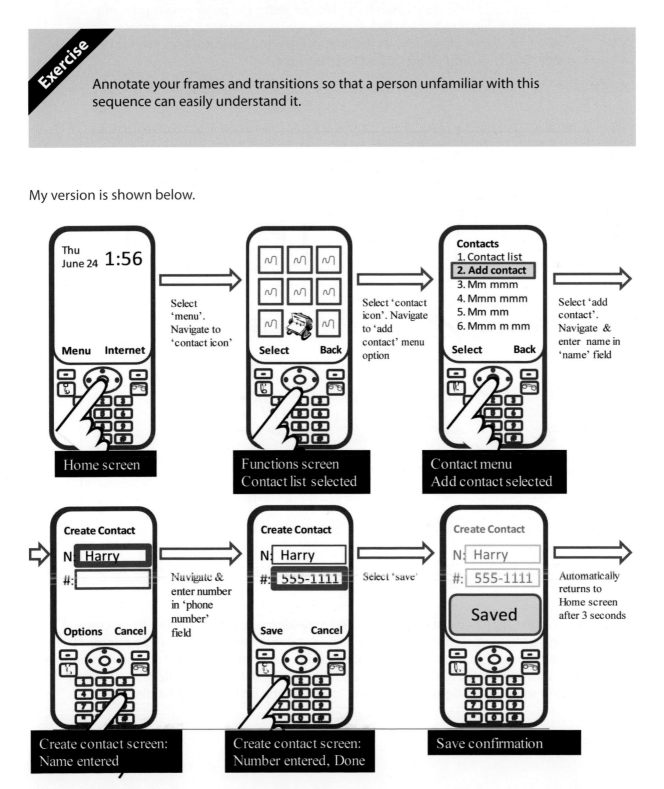

Exercise

In Chapter 3.4, we introduced an interactive shopping system. Let's detail this a bit more, and create a storyboard of it. The context is a real store. People can walk into the store, where they see paper catalogs situated next to computers. As they browse the catalog and see something they want to buy, they can scan (using a bar code reader) particular items from the catalog, which displays the items on the screen. When they place an order, the order details print out and they bring it to a sales clerk who then retrieves the items from a store room. Using the sketch shown in Chapter 3.4 as the basic design, construct a storyboard showing a person buying a blue stroller.

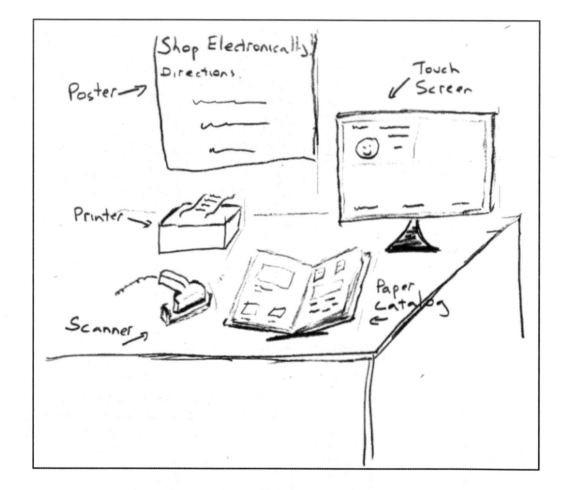

In my solution I first sketched out what the person may see in the store: a table with a screen, a poster showing getting started instructions, a paper catalog, a hand scanner, and a printer. I then used PowerPoint (again) to construct a storyboard around a template, where I copied that template to successive slides and filled in the details of each key frame. I also used sketches and 'found objects' to fill in some of the details: clip art and images found on the web (Chapter 2.3).

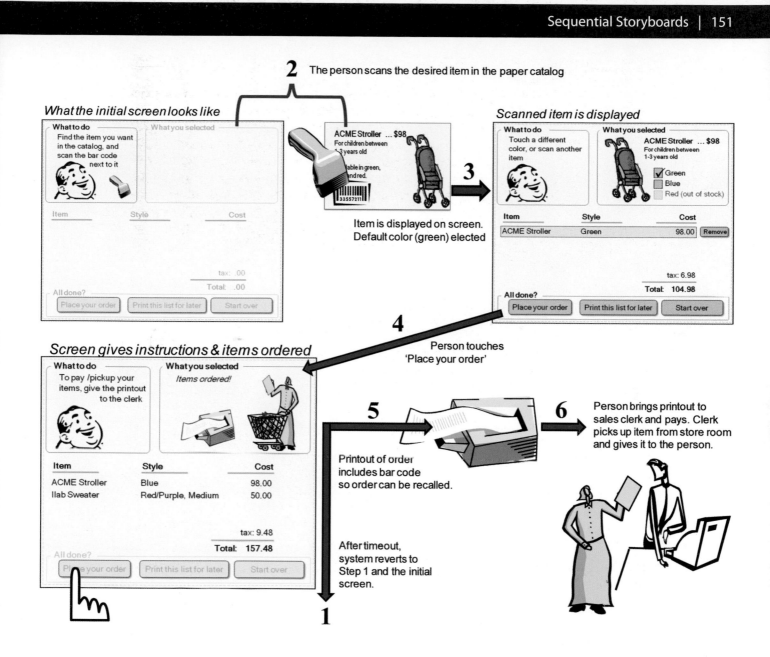

Note that this storyboard has somewhat of a hodge-podge appearance due to the different clipart and photographs used and the cramped space available to make this sequence fit in this book's page size. Yet it suffices to capture – as a storyboard sketch – the essence of this sequence. I can always beautify this later if needed.

YOU NOW KNOW

Sequential storyboarding is a commonly used technique that tells a visual story of a user experience sequence unfolding over time. The key challenge in storyboarding is to decide what sketches to include as key frames, and whether viewers can mentally fill in the space – the transitions – between these frames. Annotating the storyboard can help here, especially by explaining the user's interactions that happened during the transitions.

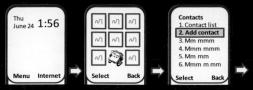

Materials

- a cell phone

- a digital watch

The sequential storyboard in the previous chapter represents a single sequential interaction episode. Sequences are appropriate for early design sketches, where you will likely focus on capturing the main series of events that occur as a person pursues his or her primary task on your imagined system.

As you move deeper into the design funnel, you will have to flesh out additional details of your selected designs, which could include:

- Adding more key frames and finer grained transitions within a sequence to illustrate exactly how the interaction happens.

- Showing the many options the person can pursue – the decision paths – at particular stages of your system.

- Showing how choosing particular options would lead to different sequences.

All this can get quite complex. One way to manage this complexity is by thinking of your storyboard as a **state transition diagram** that captures **states**, **transitions**, and **decision paths**, as well as the many ways that one can draw these states and transitions.

A STORYBOARD AS STATES AND TRANSITIONS

As a sequence, each step in the storyboard represents a single (possibly labeled) **transition** from one **state** to another. A **state** usual represents a moment in time during the interaction. A **transition** is what triggers a change in state, where transitions are typically triggered by one or more user actions. Combining these into a sequence creates a **transition diagram**.

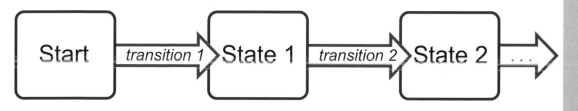

You have many options on how you can sketch these states and transitions; some are shown below. Illustrations are variations of the cell phone exercise presented previously in Chapter 4.1.

1 **The Abstract State Transition Diagram.** You can use text labels and annotations to describe each state as an abstraction. This is appropriate for early designs, where you are trying to sketch out the flow of user activities as a person uses the system to do a task, without having to detail (or commit to) what the interface would necessarily look like.

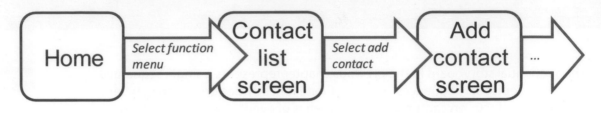

2 **The Visual Interface State Transition Diagram.** You can sketch the appearance of the interface itself as it passes through each state. This gives very rich information, as it is a highly literal diagram. It is appropriate when you are trying to flesh out the fine-grained details of the interface as the task progresses. But it also demands that you have a pretty good idea of what the system looks like at each state, as it will be a bit harder to modify if you change your mind.

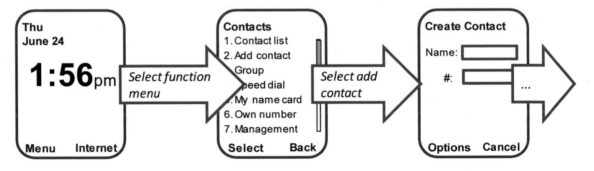

3 **The Annotated State Transition Diagram.** The state diagram is augmented to include explanatory text. You can annotate each state and transition as much as you want. This example shows the above visual interface state transition diagram with annotations.

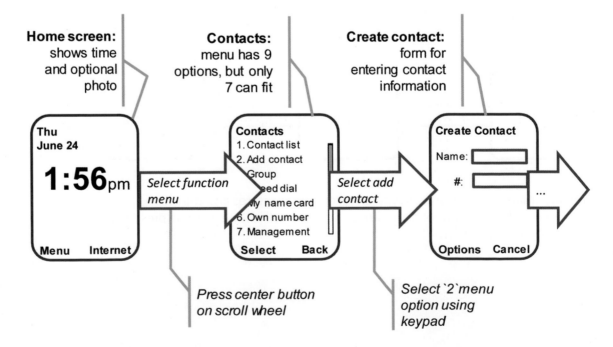

The Indexed State Transition Diagram. This combines the above methods. The diagram resembles the abstraction, but it also includes indexes to other figures. Those other figures could show:

- what the screen(s) look like in that state (as in the Visual Interface Diagram), which is the technique shown in the figures below,

- explanatory text that explains the abstraction,

- another more detailed transition diagram,

- decisions that could be made at that point that lead to alternate sequences (as we will show in the next section).

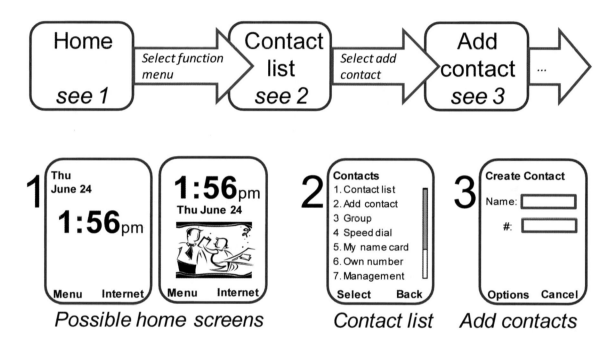

While the particular approach you will use depends on your needs, you will invariably find yourself using indexes to define most complex storyboards. This is because:

- you can generate multiple sketches as variations for what happens at that index (to illustrate, the figure above includes two possibilities of what the cell phone's home screen at index 1 could look like),

- they help you manage complexity that is bound to occur when developing large state transition diagrams.

This chapter elaborates the previously introduced concepts of storyboarding by illustrating examples of branching storyboards, that is, state transition diagrams showing decision paths as transitions. It applies what you've learned about state transition diagrams to the cell phone and interactive shopping system examples.

THE CELL PHONE EXAMPLE

In Chapter 4.1, you sketched out a sequence that captured how a phone's interaction unfolds over time as you enter a person into the phone's contact list. Using your cell phone, revisit that sequence, but this time show a few of the other decision paths a person can make along the way. In particular:

The Abstract State Transition Diagram
As before, look at how your cell phone lets you add a contact. This time, sketch an abstract state transition diagram showing alternate paths you could take along the way. Show at least several states and these major decision paths as transitions and states that occur as you move through your phone's interface to the contact list.

My solution is shown below. First, I show the choices available on the Functions screen (my phone displays 7 selectable icons), the Contacts screen (7 menu options), the Add contacts screen (1 option button)

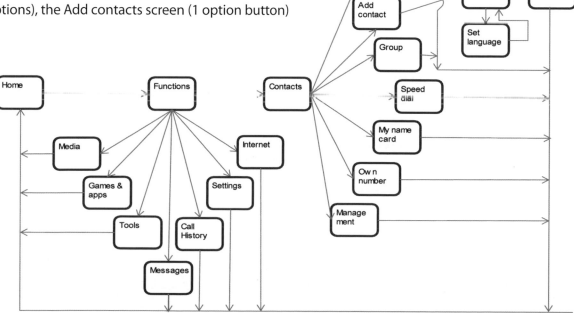

and the Create contact screen (2 options). I also show how all these choices eventually lead back to the Home screen. Of course, much information is left out, but it does show the navigational phone (at least in part).

The Visual Interface State Transition Diagram
Based on your previous exercise, sketch a visual interface state transition diagram showing at least one state and all the decision paths coming out of it to another state.

My solution below begins with the 'contacts' state above, where I sketched the appearance of the contacts menu and its seven items. I then sketched the transitions to the seven states that would be displayed by selecting each menu item, where I sketched the appearance of the screens in those seven states.

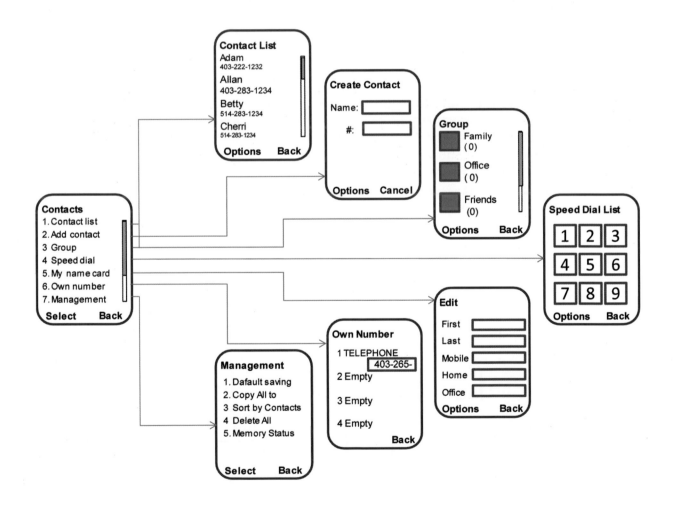

The Indexed State Transition Diagram
Convert your sketch in the previous exercise into an indexed state transition diagram. First, show the visual interface within your chosen state. Second, draw all the transitions (decisions paths) coming out of that state, with the new states drawn as indexes. Third, take one of those new indexed states and sketch another separate visual interface transition diagram showing its details.

The solution below is similar to the previous one. The top diagram shows the same contact screen as a state, but now the seven menu options are shown as transitions leading to indexes. Each index is a pointer to another diagram. I show only one of these other diagrams at the bottom, where index 2 is illustrated in full as a partially annotated visual interface transition diagram.

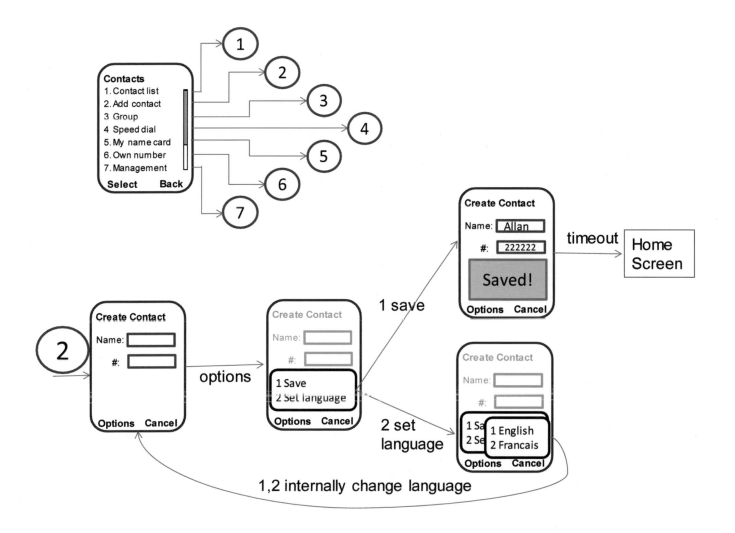

THE INTERACTIVE SHOPPING SYSTEM EXAMPLE

In the previous chapter, we introduced the primary sequence of the interactive shopping system, where we illustrated how a person could buy a single item. We will continue this exercise by developing it into a branching storyboard.

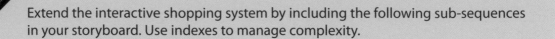

Exercise Extend the interactive shopping system by including the following sub-sequences in your storyboard. Use indexes to manage complexity.

- **Multiple items.** A person scans in two or more items.
- **Modifying items on the list.**
  – A person removes one or more of the items in the list.
  – A person changes a previously entered item's property (e.g., its color).
- **Comparison shopping.** A person prints out the list without purchasing anything, and then comes back at a later time to buy the items on it (a bar code specifying this particular order is part of the printout).
- **Not buying anything.** The person can cancel this order explicitly, or just walk away.

My solution is shown on the following page. Note that these storyboards almost completely define the behavior of this interactive system.

The first storyboard provides an overview map. It describes how only one option (scanning an item) is available from the initial home screen #1, which leads to the order screen (state #2). It also shows all the basic states #3–7 reachable from this main order screen. These are done as indexes. The storyboards that follow explain what happens at those indexes Storyboard 3 also has another index to state #8, as it only makes sense when two or more items are shown on the order screen.

1 Basic Operation

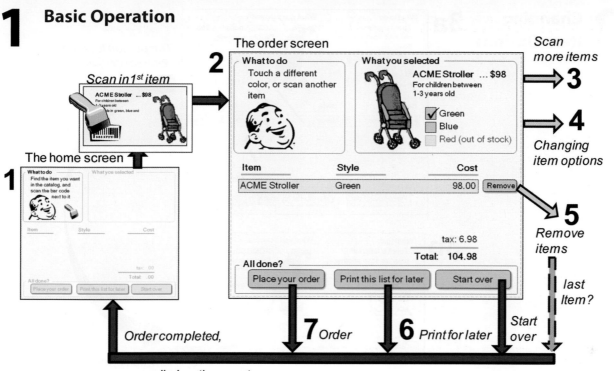

Scan in 1st item

The home screen

The order screen

Scan more items → **3**

→ **4**
Changing item options

2

What to do
Touch a different color, or scan another item

What you selected
ACME Stroller ... $98
For children between 1-3 years old
☑ Green
☐ Blue
☐ Red (out of stock)

Item	Style	Cost	
ACME Stroller	Green	98.00	Remove

tax: 6.98
Total: 104.98

All done?
Place your order | Print this list for later | Start over

5
Remove items

last Item?

Order completed, cancelled, or times out

7 *Order* **6** *Print for later* *Start over*

2 Scanning in Multiple Items

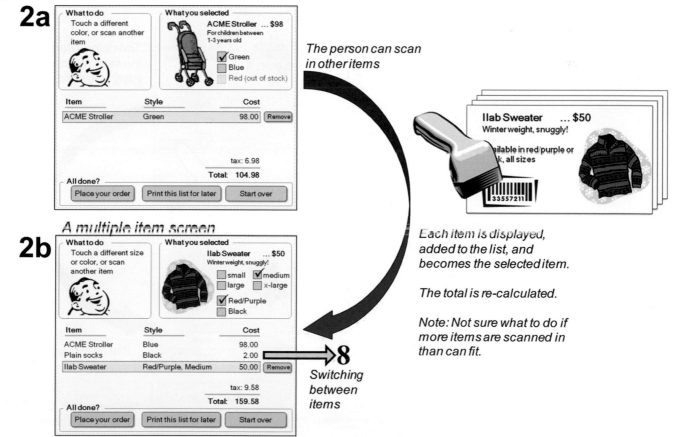

2a

What to do
Touch a different color, or scan another item

What you selected
ACME Stroller ... $98
For children between 1-3 years old
☑ Green
☐ Blue
☐ Red (out of stock)

Item	Style	Cost	
ACME Stroller	Green	98.00	Remove

tax: 6.98
Total: 104.98

All done?
Place your order | Print this list for later | Start over

The person can scan in other items

Ilab Sweater ... $50
Winter weight, snuggly!
...ailable in red/purple or ...k, all sizes

Each item is displayed, added to the list, and becomes the selected item.

The total is re-calculated.

Note: Not sure what to do if more items are scanned in than can fit.

A multiple item screen

2b

What to do
Touch a different size or color, or scan another item

What you selected
Ilab Sweater ... $50
Winter weight, snuggly!
☐ small ☑ medium
☐ large ☐ x-large
☑ Red/Purple
☐ Black

Item	Style	Cost	
ACME Stroller	Blue	98.00	
Plain socks	Black	2.00	
Ilab Sweater	Red/Purple, Medium	50.00	Remove

tax: 9.58
Total: 159.58

All done?
Place your order | Print this list for later | Start over

8
Switching between items

3 Changing Item Options

3a

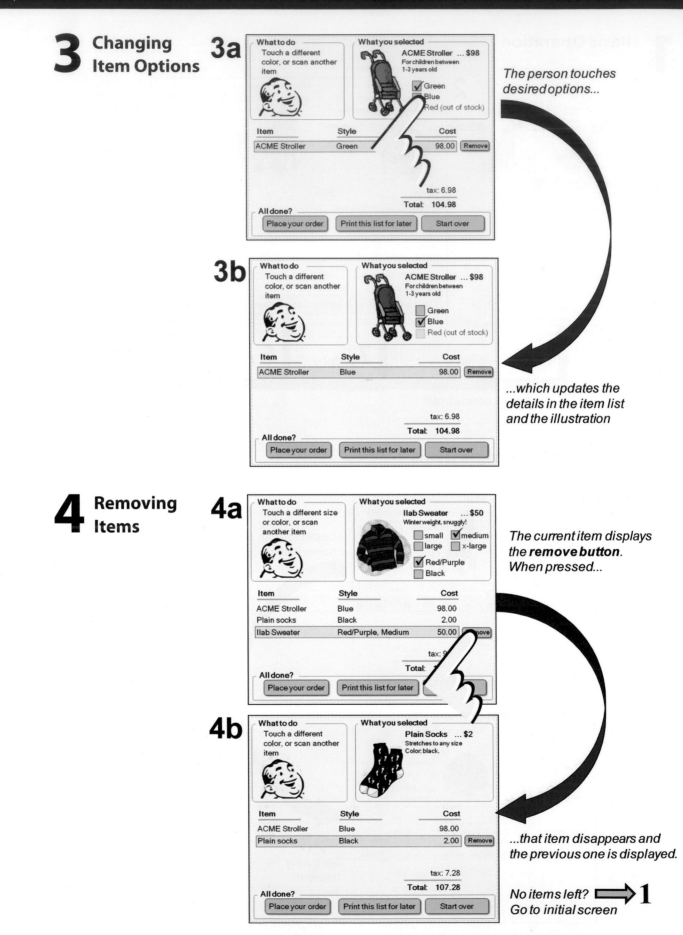

What to do
Touch a different color, or scan another item

What you selected
ACME Stroller ... $98
For children between 1-3 years old

☑ Green
☐ Blue
☐ Red (out of stock)

Item	Style	Cost	
ACME Stroller	Green	98.00	Remove

tax: 6.98
Total: 104.98

All done?
[Place your order] [Print this list for later] [Start over]

The person touches desired options...

3b

What to do
Touch a different color, or scan another item

What you selected
ACME Stroller ... $98
For children between 1-3 years old

☐ Green
☑ Blue
☐ Red (out of stock)

Item	Style	Cost	
ACME Stroller	Blue	98.00	Remove

tax: 6.98
Total: 104.98

All done?
[Place your order] [Print this list for later] [Start over]

...which updates the details in the item list and the illustration

4 Removing Items

4a

What to do
Touch a different size or color, or scan another item

What you selected
Ilab Sweater ... $50
Winter weight, snuggly!

☐ small ☑ medium
☐ large ☐ x-large

☑ Red/Purple
☐ Black

Item	Style	Cost	
ACME Stroller	Blue	98.00	
Plain socks	Black	2.00	
Ilab Sweater	Red/Purple, Medium	50.00	Remove

tax: 9
Total:

All done?
[Place your order] [Print this list for later]

*The current item displays the **remove button**. When pressed...*

4b

What to do
Touch a different color, or scan another item

What you selected
Plain Socks ... $2
Stretches to any size
Color: black.

Item	Style	Cost	
ACME Stroller	Blue	98.00	
Plain socks	Black	2.00	Remove

tax: 7.28
Total: 107.28

All done?
[Place your order] [Print this list for later] [Start over]

...that item disappears and the previous one is displayed.

No items left? ➡ **1**
Go to initial screen

5 Print for Later

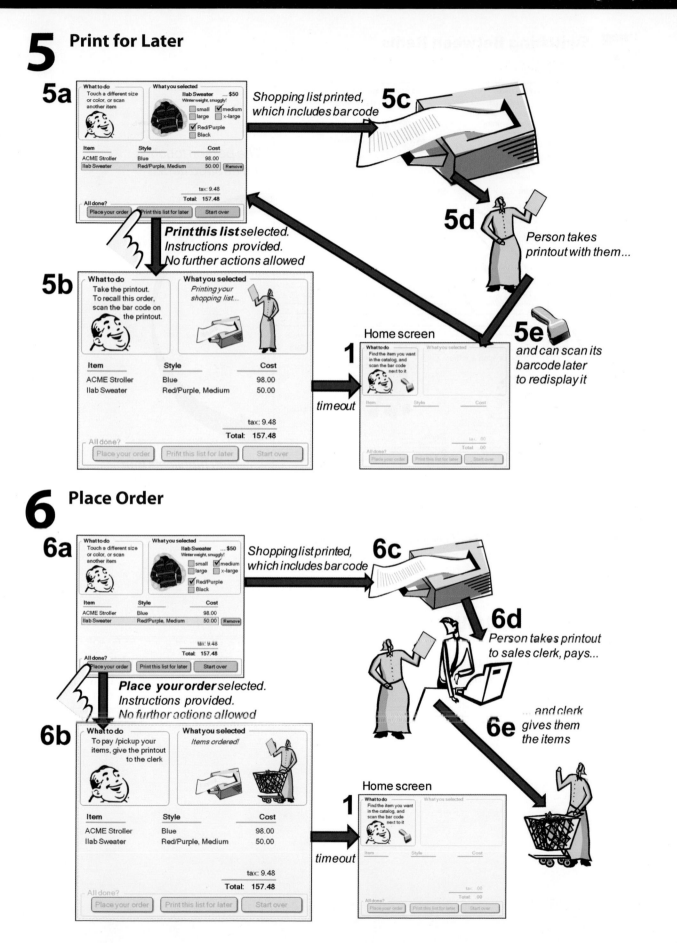

5a

Shopping list printed, which includes bar code

5c

5d

Print this list selected.
Instructions provided.
No further actions allowed

5b

Person takes
printout with them...

Home screen

timeout

5e and can scan its
barcode later
to redisplay it

6 Place Order

6a

Shopping list printed, which includes bar code

6c

6d

Person takes printout
to sales clerk, pays...

Place your order selected.
Instructions provided.
No further actions allowed

6b

...and clerk
6e gives them
the items

Home screen

timeout

7 Switching Between Items

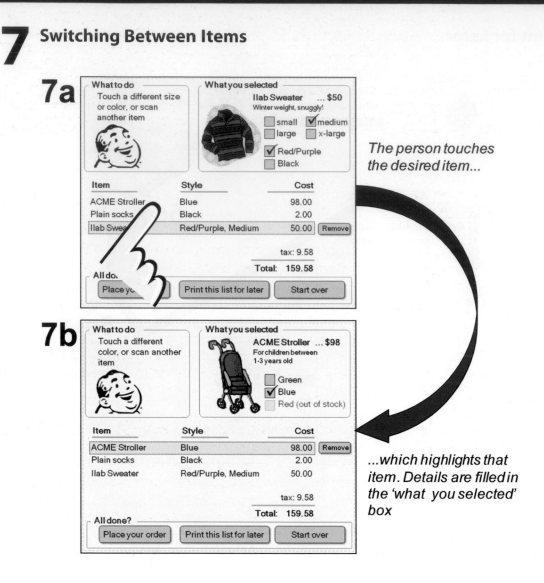

7a

7b

The person touches the desired item...

...which highlights that item. Details are filled in the 'what you selected' box

YOU NOW KNOW

This chapter illustrated two examples of branching storyboards. They used a combination of techniques to try to manage complexity when showing a multitude of decision paths and possible states.

The storyboards featured so far present snapshots of the user interface. But the interface is only part of the story that occurs as people interact: what is missing is context. The narrative storyboard provides this context. It uses a sequence of images to tell a more complete story about people's interaction over time, where each image in the storyboard represents a particular event. They communicate information about the location where the interaction takes place, present the people as personalities, and provide details about the other actions and things people are doing as they interact. As Laurie Vertelney (1998) points out, narrative storyboards are actually a variation of the cinematographic storyboard found in planning movies, except applied to interaction design.

After introducing some vocabulary, we present two alternative techniques for creating narrative storyboards: **sketching stories by hand** or **using photos as source material**.

A VOCABULARY OF CAMERA SHOTS AND FILM MAKING

Film makers use specific terminology to describe the composition of a certain scene within a storyboard. We use some of their terms to describe the scenes in our sketched storyboards, and you can use those terms to think about how you want to compose and vary your own narrative images. A partial list of popular **camera shots** is provided below; a more complete description of these and other terms is found in Katz 1991 and Block 2007.

Extreme long shot (wide shot)
A view showing details of the setting, location, etc.

Long shot
Showing the full height of a person.

Medium shot
Shows a person's head and shoulders.

Over-the-shoulder shot
Looking over the shoulder of a person.

Point of view shot (POV)
Seeing everything a person sees.

Close-up
such as showing details of a user interface on a device the person is holding.

Continue the storyline sketches with appropriate camera shots
Now continue with the remaining sketches of the storyboard. Apply the simple sketching techniques we introduced in earlier chapters. Use stick figures to illustrate people's postures and orientation (Chapter 3.3), or draw simple silhouettes of people and objects with the photo tracing technique (Chapter 3.9). Our five sketches are shown below.

1. Person passing by an advertisement board

2. Notices one announcement and is interested in more information

3. Taking a photo of a barcode on the poster.

4. The mobile phone downloads detailed information about the new product.

5. The person puts away the phone and turns around.

In each of the above sketched scenes you can apply the cinematographic techniques of varying camera shots. For the beginning and end we used the extreme wide shot to illustrate context. The over-the-shoulder view in the second frame shows details of the person and the board, as this emphasizes what the person is looking at. We then used the first person point of view shot in frame 3 to emphasize the action a person is doing (i.e., taking a photo of the bar code). Finally, the close-up in frame 4 allows us to show details of the information displayed on the screen.

5 Emphasize actions and motions

If needed, you can now add visual annotations to the sketches. Annotations (drawn in yellow below) are a valuable way of indicating and emphasizing important motions or actions that are otherwise difficult to show in a static image.

1. Person passing by an advertisement board

2. Notices one announcement and is interested in more information

3. Taking a photo of a barcode on the poster.

4. The mobile phone downloads detailed information about the new product.

5. The person puts away the phone and turns around.

For example, we used various arrows to indicate a person's motion.

In our establishing scene, we drew a large arrow on the floor indicating that the person is walking by the announcement board.

In the 2nd frame, the circling arrow emphasizes the head-turning motion of the person just noticing something of interest on the board.

The last frame also uses a large arrow, this time showing the person walking away.

Section 5 ⟩⟩

Animating the User Experience

When a storyboard has fine-grained transitions that visually lead from one step to the next, you can transform the storyboard into an interactive movie. Such animations provide a visual narrative by playing back a story, or by illustrating different branches in a story.

5.1   **The Animated Sequence** explains how to animate a single interaction sequence as a slide show through image registration

5.2   **Motion Paths** shows you how you can animate graphical movement, such as the cursor, across frames. This emphasizes the illusion of smooth interaction

5.3   **Branching Animations** use hyperlinks to simulate interactions at certain branch points, where each can trigger different paths in your animation

5.4   **Keyframes and Tweening** are two very powerful ways you can create animations that illustrate highly interactive interfaces

5.5   **Linear Video** demonstrates how video and video editing tools can help you rapidly create an animation from paper-based sketches

The last section showed how an interaction sequence can unfold by showing successive frames as a storyboard. In essence, *time* unfolds over *space*. Another approach is to *animate* the sequence, where the story unfolds by displaying successive frames in the same location over time. That is, the animated sequence becomes a movie.

THE SLIDE SHOW

Chapter 3.6 described how presentation tools such as PowerPoint can simplify the task of creating individual sketches. Presentation tools are also very suitable for creating an **animated sequence**. The idea is simple: you create your storyboard as a sequence of successive PowerPoint frames. Then you go into slideshow mode to animate the sequence. But to make this work, you first need to know about the **registration problem**, and how to solve it by **registering images**.

THE REGISTRATION PROBLEM

Imagine the simple interface below (an equipment rental system), shown as a storyboard illustrating a person's interaction while renting a pair of gloves and a jacket.

Materials

Slideware or equivalent presentation software

For example,

– Microsoft PowerPoint

– Apple Keynote

Equipment Rental

Rent outerwear all winter for cheap. Stay warm this snowy season!

Choose clothes

frame 1

Equipment Rental

☐	Gloves	3.00
☐	Hat	2.00
☐	Jacket	5.00
	Total	0.00

Check out

frame 2

Equipment Rental

☑	Gloves	3.00
☐	Hat	2.00
☐	Jacket	5.00
	Total	3.00

Check out

frame 3

Equipment Rental

☑	Gloves	3.00
☐	Hat	2.00
☑	Jacket	5.00
	Total	8.00

Check out

frame 4

Equipment Rental

☑	Gloves	3.00
☐	Hat	2.00
☑	Jacket	5.00
	Total	8.00

Check out

frame 5

Equipment Rental

You have rented **gloves** and a **jacket**.

Go to the counter, pay **$8.00**, and pick up your clothes.

Done

frame 6

You want to animate this scene by using these images as frames. Each frame will be a slide in a slide deck in your presentation tool. We animate them by playing the slide deck as a slide show.

But what would happen if each image was in a slightly different position on each slide? The images would jump around, and the illusion of animation would be broken. For example, if we take the first four frames and simply place them atop each other without paying attention to aligning them, we may get something similar to what is shown below. This clearly won't work, as the viewer doesn't expect the static elements in the image – the window frame, its title, the position of unchanging content – to jump around between frames.

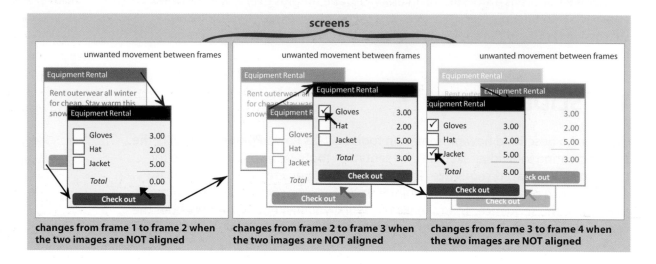

THE SOLUTION: REGISTERING IMAGES

The easiest way to solve the registration problem is to create a series of templates, where static items are always in the same fixed position on the slide (templates were introduced in Chapter 3.8). You would then modify these templates to create your actual frames. As long as you don't move the fixed items around, your static items will then appear in the same place in your animated sequence.

1 **Create a Master Frame Template**
Create a master template that contains only those elements that are constant in each frame – the lowest common denominator of graphical items across frames. This will help you create other templates.

In our example interface, this will comprise the window itself, its title bar and title text, as well as the button and its text. We also specified some key positions of some items relative to another. First, we marked the upper left corner of the frame (or screen) edge, and specified the position of the window relative to that corner. This ensures that the window will always appear in the same spot on the frame. Second, we marked the window content margins at the left and right part of the window, because we always want the window contents to appear within this fixed margin.

Finally, because we will make copies of this template, we can expect the sizes and positions of all these elements will stay in the same place. Just in case, we've annotated the template with several key positions and sizes.

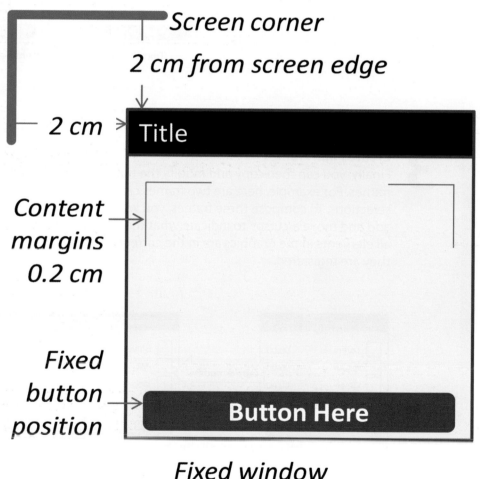

2 **Create Specialized Frame Templates**
You can now refine the master template to make more specialized frame templates. Within a presentation tool such as PowerPoint, all you have to do is copy the slide holding the master frame template, and then edit that copy accordingly.

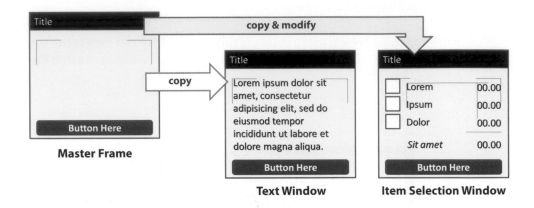

Master Frame **Text Window** **Item Selection Window**

3 **Create Final Frames**
Finally, you can then copy and modify the template to create your final frames. For example, here are two frames created from the template for item selections. To compose these frames, you would just edit the existing text, and add and move a 'cursor' to indicate what the user has selected. The key is that all elements in the graphics are in the correct position across all frames, i.e., they are registered.

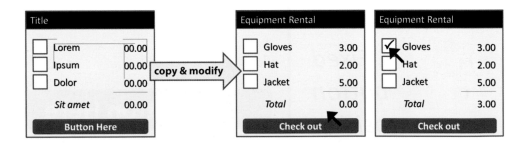

4

Place Each Frame in the Desired Sequence in Your Presentation Software
Because each frame is just a copy of a template, and because items are in constant locations, all you need to do now is place the frames in the order you want them played out as a sequence. This should be the same as your storyboard. For example, this is what the sequence looks like in PowerPoint. The left bar shows each frame in the sequence.

Tips

You can use the 'speaking notes' facility in a presentation tool to annotate your frames. For example, the bottom region in the figure explains what this particular frame is for.

While we illustrate our example using slideware, registering images can be used for other forms of media. Chapter 5.5 illustrates how the same technique can apply in video production.

Other Animation Tools

Presentation tools are primarily for creating slide shows; animations were added to them as another way to craft compelling presentations. While simple animations can be added to your sequence, complex ones tend to be either impossible because the tool doesn't support them, or hard to do.

If you regularly design scripted slide shows (see Chapter 6.4), or if you are interested in complex animations, you should learn an animation tool specifically designed to animate graphics, suc as Adobe's Flash. While the learning curve is higher than a presentation tool, such applications provide far more creative power (we show a few in Chapter 5.4). The danger is that you will spend your time creating lovely animations rather than developing your ideas. Remember the role of your sketch!

3 Creating the Motion Path

The next step is to draw a line that indicates the actual path of movement of the cursor. You do this simply by drawing a line from the center of the cursor to the center of the other cursor. After this is done (and checking to make sure the animation works), you can remove the reference cursor you had pasted in.

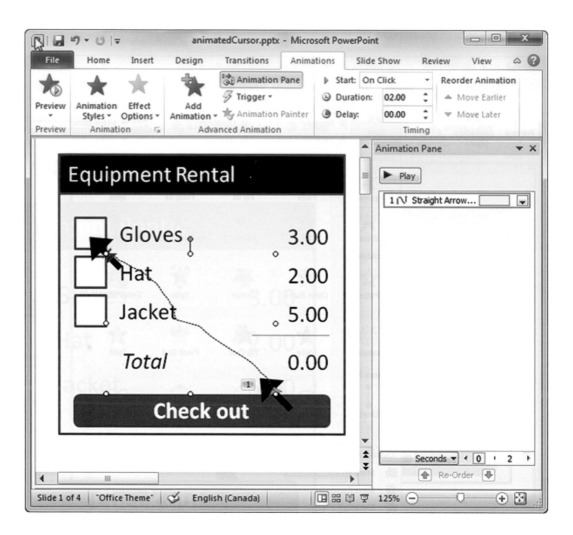

4 Adding Effects

At this point (and depending on your software), you can further control the animation. In PowerPoint, I can select the animation in the animation pane (on the right side) and raise a menu and control panel window that gives me this control. For example, I can control when the animation starts, and how slowly or quickly the animation plays (via its timing).

I can also add a variety of effects to the animation. In this case, I added a clicking sound to this animation, to emulate the user clicking the 'Gloves' checkbox.

YOU NOW KNOW

Motion paths let you animate graphical items, such as a cursor, as you switch between frames. When used effectively, it increases the viewers' feeling that they are watching a movie of someone interacting with your system.

Chapter 4.3 illustrated how storyboards can have multiple branches (or interaction paths), where the particular path taken at a branch point usually depends on the particular action of an end user. This chapter explains how – unlike a normal movie or slide show – you can create sketch animations that allow different paths to be taken as the animation runs.

SELECTING ALTERNATIVE INTERACTION PATHS THROUGH HYPERLINKS

Many slide presentation systems allow you to embed a **hyperlink** into or atop of particular graphics or regions of a slide. While the hyperlink can point to many things, for our purposes we will use a hyperlink that references another slide in the current slide deck.

The best way to illustrate this is to try it yourself. Our first example, illustrated below, will be a trivial sketch across three slides, with each slide representing a different system state. Slide 1 contains two 'buttons'. Depending on which button you click, different text will then be displayed. As suggested by the arrows below, clicking 'Say Hello' will display slide 2, while clicking 'Say Goodbye' will display slide 3.

1 Create the three slides below (I used PowerPoint). The first slide is just two rectangles with some text in them, while the other two just contain the given text.

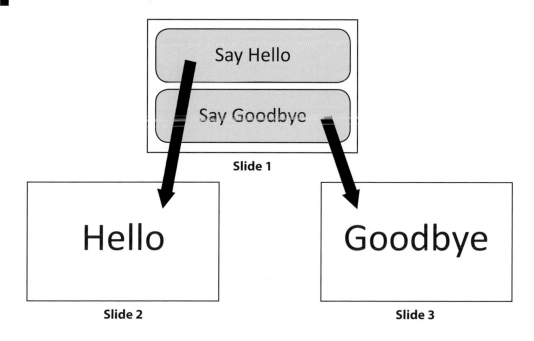

Slide 1

Slide 2

Slide 3

Materials

Slide presentation software that lets you:

– hyperlink from an area or object on one slide to another slide

Microsoft PowerPoint is an example of such a system, but there are many others available that you can use.

2 Add a hyperlink to the 'Say Hello' rectangle, which links to slide 2. In my version of PowerPoint, you do this by right-clicking over the 'Say Hello' rectangle to raise the context menu, and then select the 'Hyperlink' option.

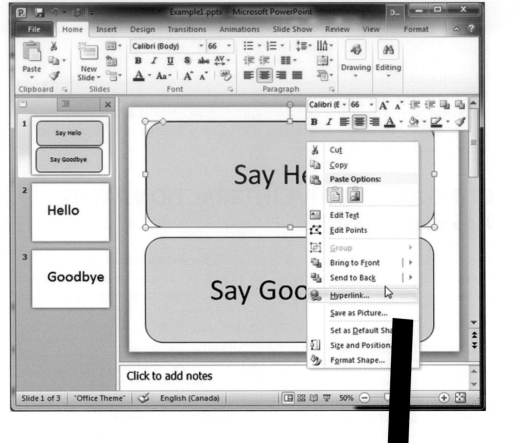

 3 This raises the dialog box below showing the kinds of things you can link to (see left side). Select the 'Place in this Document' button, and then select slide 2 containing the text 'Hello'.

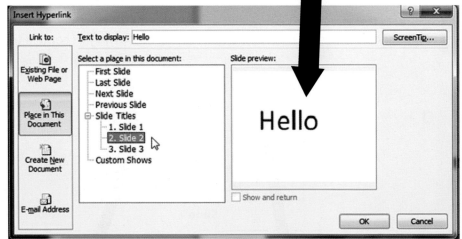

4 Similarly, add a hyperlink to the 'Say Goodbye' rectangle, except this time make the hyperlink point to slide 3.

5 Play your slide show; clicking each button should jump to the appropriate slide.

Tip

Animating indexed state transition diagrams
Hyperlinks can also link to other slide decks. This means you can put sub-sequences into individual slide decks. Your 'master' slide deck can then index these sequences. This helps manage complexity. It also means you can develop alternative sub-sequences that can be accessed simply by changing the hyperlink.

Example: A Complete Branching Animation

Reconsider our example equipment rental system you saw in Chapter 5.1. There are three types of screens: the initial splash screen, the rental screen, and the final payment screen. Try (on your own) to create a branching animation that illustrates the results of all possible interactions. In essence, you are creating a fully detailed state transition diagram, showing the effects of all user operations. Make sure to include what happens when you click on all buttons and checkboxes. Also include unclicking boxes that you may have checked previously (i.e., an 'undo' operation).

Hint: Create versions of all screen possibilities, order them in your slide deck, and then add the necessary hyperlinks.

Solution

The screens below realize all possibilities as a branching animation. The numbered arrows next to each interactive element (the buttons and checkboxes) indicate the hyperlink, i.e., it shows what screen would be displayed if a person clicked in that interactive element. For example, in slide 2, clicking the 'Gloves' checkbox would go to slide 3. However, clicking the 'Hat' checkbox in slide 2 would go to slide 4 instead. Undo also happens. In slide 3, clicking the 'Gloves' checkbox goes back to Slide 2; that is, it is the same as unchecking the box. In slides 2 through 9, clicking 'Checkout' leads to a variety of different slides, as the text content of the screen depends on what items had been selected. In Slides 11–17, clicking the 'Done' button always return to the initial slide 1.

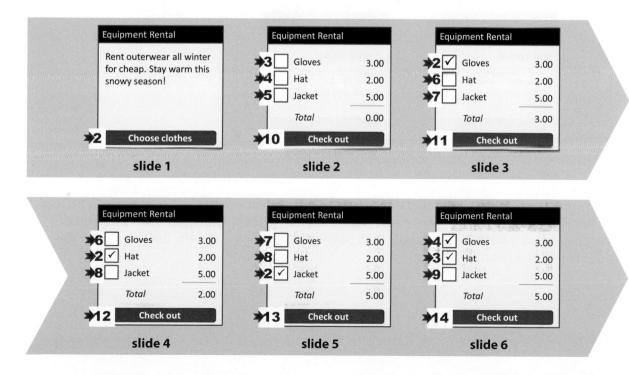

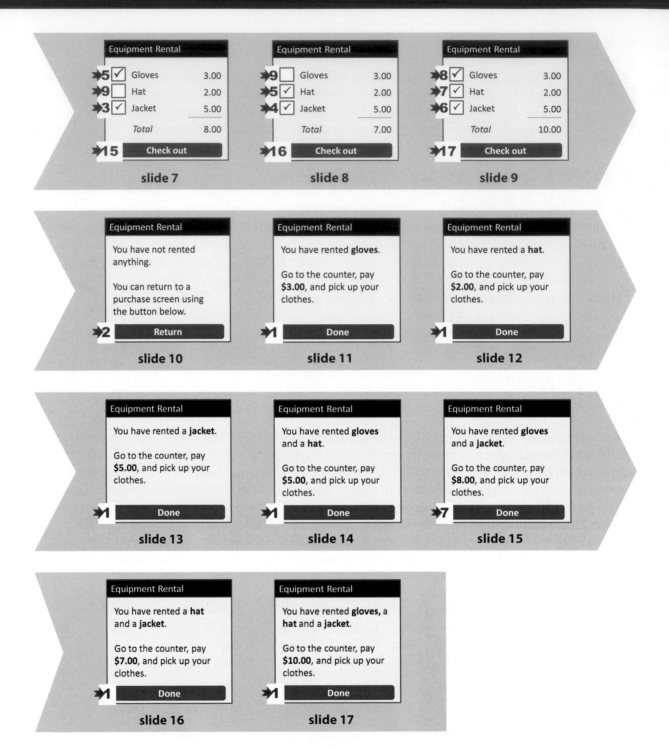

The advantage of having a fully operational branching sequence is that you or someone else can operate the interface as if it were real. No direction is needed, as all options work. Another advantage is that it forces you to consider all possible paths in your system. But see the tip: this is a double-edged sword.

Tips

Are You Feeling Overwhelmed?

Our simple example required you to create the 17 different screens, and to add 33 hyperlinks. This is clearly tedious, even with templates. It is also impractical if you are sketching a system that is feature-rich.

The solution to this is to only instrument a few key paths, i.e., enough to illustrate your idea. Remember, this is a sketch, and a sketch is about ideas. For example, you may want to show how one goes from the splash screen (slide 1), to the main order screen (slide 2), and how one can select and unselect one or two items (e.g., slide 3 and slide 7), and an example of how one can place the order (slide 15) or what happens when no items are selected (slide 10). All other paths are so similar that little benefit is gained from 'implementing' them in the animation.

The basic strategy is to animate just enough of your sketch paths to illustrate the breadth of different features in your system, while going into just enough depth to illustrate the functionality of those features. Jacob Nielsen calls this **Horizontal** (breadth) vs. **Vertical** (depth) **prototyping**. (He also describes a **Scenario**, which is a single scripted path through your sketch – this is equivalent to a sequential animation.) Your selection of animation paths don't even have to do both – your sketch animation may only explore the functionality of a single feature in depth, but not other features. Or you may want to give an overall 'look and feel' of your system by showing the different features, without going into depth about the actual functionality of any one of them.

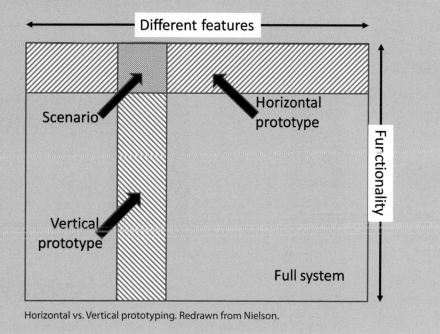

Horizontal vs. Vertical prototyping. Redrawn from Nielson.

References

Nielsen, J. (1993) *Usability Engineering*. Morgan-Kaufmann. See the chapter on The Usability Engineering Lifecycle, pp. 94–95.

YOU NOW KNOW

Branching animations can be implemented easily using hyperlinks in slide presentation systems, where the branch taken depends on the hyperlink selected. You can use these animations to illustrate different high level portions of your system (horiziontal prototyping) or to go into depth of a portion of your system (vertical prototyping), or a combination of the two.

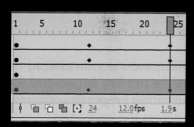

A few chapters back, we illustrated how you could use motion paths within PowerPoint to create a simple motion path that moves an object around a screen. However, most presentation tools are not really designed to support the more complex animated sketches you may want to create. This is where a tool designed for multimedia animation creation – such as Adobe Flash – can help. While this means extra cost for the software and time to learn it, many advantages accrue.

- You will be able to create complex animations of highly interactive scenarios reasonably quickly.

- You will be able to articulate fine details of how the interaction unfolds over time.

- Most systems let you quickly render animations as stand-alone videos.

- The result can be far more professional looking and detailed, to the point that your system may appear 'real'.

It is beyond the scope of this book to teach you how to use a multimedia animation tool, especially because each tool will have its own set of features and idiosyncratic interface for creating animations. However, almost all will include two fundamental capabilities: **keyframes** and **inbetweening** (also known as **tweening**).

We'll provide and illustrate several definitions by animating an imagined photo viewer that runs on a touch-sensitive digital table. Similar to photo apps on smart phones, the idea is that a person can select and enlarge a photo with two fingers as he brings it into the table's center.

SOME DEFINITIONS

Keyframe: An important frame that defines the start and/or end frame in a particular animation sequence. Each keyframe contains objects as well as the current properties of that object, such as an object's position, size, orientation, color, and so on. These properties can vary across keyframes.

Animation properties: Any property of an animation that can be specified as differences between keyframes, where that property can be animated over time. Typical properties include basic object transformations (scale, rotation, movement), advanced transformation (object skewing, transforming one shape into a completely different shape), visual properties (color transforms, fading, transparency), and more.

Materials

- Adobe Flash or equivalent multimedia animation system

EXAMPLE: ADOBE FLASH

Let's create the above animation in Adobe Flash CS4. What is shown below is not necessarily the best way to do it, nor are all details provided. However, it suffices to illustrate the basic idea.

1 **Create a stage (the backdrop for your animation) and populate it with your visual elements.**
I opened a stage – the area containing the animation – where I set it to run at 12 frames per second. I found clipart of a finger on the web, and I grabbed 4 personal photos. I imported all these into Flash (making two copies of the finger). I then resized and placed them on the stage. Using each item's context menu, I converted them into symbols, a type of object that Flash knows how to animate. We now have keyframe 1.

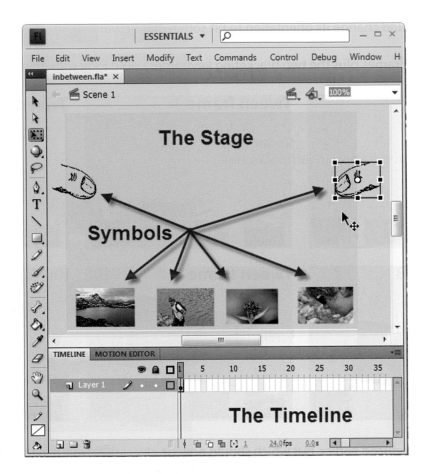

As seen in the image above, this process is somewhat similar (so far) to how we would lay out objects in slideware or drawing application. The key difference is the appearance of the timeline at the bottom of the window, which allows objects on particular layers to be animated over time. We are currently looking at frame 1, where 37 frames (~3 seconds) are visible in the timeline. The first frame is always a keyframe, as indicated by the black circle in the '1' square on the timeline.

2   Create tweened frames filling up 1 second of the animation.

In Adobe Flash, you can create a per-symbol frame for each object you want to animate by creating a Motion Tween for it. This is done via each symbol's context menu, as shown here. As you do this, the timeline will add a layer for each symbol in the timeline, and extend the timeline to include 1 second (12 frames) of animation. If you run the animation, though, you won't see anything happening as all symbols are in the same place.

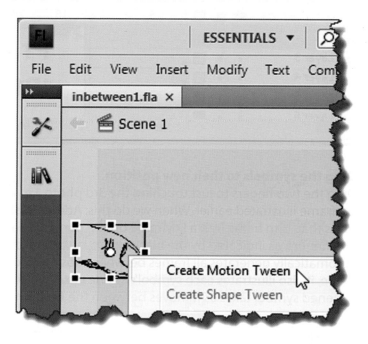

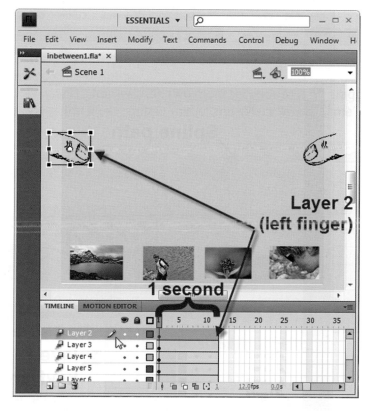

7 Create the third keyframe.

Moving to frame 24 and similar to Step 4, reposition the fingers and the picture. Also change the orientation of the right finger and the image, and resize the image as needed. As before, the tweened frames will be automatically created.

However, you will now see a problem: the photo will start animating from the 2nd frame on, which is not what we wanted. This is because no keyframe exists at frame 12 for the photo on layer 5. To correct this, move the frame indicator to frame 12, raise the context menu on layer 5, and select *'Insert Keyframe'*. Because the position of the image between frames 1 and 12 is unchanged, the tweening to Frame 24 will now begin on frame 13.

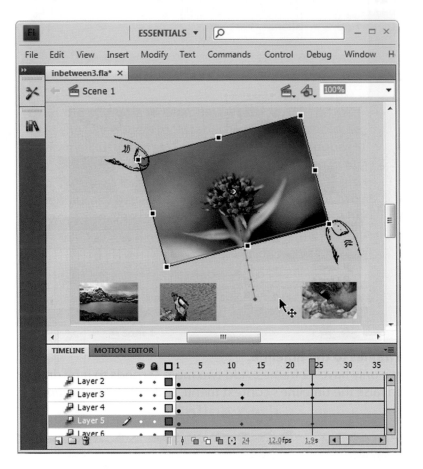

8 Create the final keyframe.

Moving to frame 36, reposition the fingers to the side of the table. This repeats what you've seen before, so we won't bother showing you what this looks like. Your animation is now complete!

YOU TRY

The above example illustrates one of the most rudimentary things you can do with a good animation package. Learn and experiment with the animation package of your choosing to try to replicate what we just did.

A good way to learn and exercise your skills at creating multimedia animations is to try to mimic a short highly interactive sequence of your choosing in some existing software system. Start with something simple, such as an animation that repositions objects, as in the photo editor above. Then move on to more challenging sequences, as these will push you into discovering advanced capabilities in your animation system. And if you are up for the challenge, you can learn how to script (or program) your animations for even more power.

Tip

Don't get caught up.
Techniques such as keyframes, tweening, and others that you will learn as you become familiar with your animation package are just other tools in your sketching toolkit. While animations can be fun to create and awesome to view, they don't suit every occasion, nor are they always necessary. Be judicious.

YOU NOW KNOW

Keyframes and tweening are two very powerful ways you can create animations that illustrate highly interactive interfaces. They do require specialized multimedia animation software, but the investment in cost and time can be well worth it.

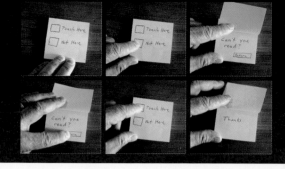

A sketch can be brought to life by creating a movie showing a continuous interaction sequence. In contrast to storyboards, where people have to imagine what happens in the transitions, movies can show those transitions while voice-overs can explain what is going on as actions are being done. Such sketches can be quite compelling, for if done well they can tell a complete story of a particular interaction sequence.

Creating a movie of an interaction sequence – a linear video – is surprisingly easy. Aside from some office supplies (see Chapter 3.7), the only specialized equipment you will need is a video camera (a home video camera should be fine), a tripod, and basic video-editing software.

PREPARATION

In this example, we create a movie by recording and then editing a person 'interacting' with a paper-based interface. Our example is simple: it uses four Post-It Notes, each representing a different screen with different interface controls as shown in step 4. Our story will show what happens when a person presses the various buttons on the first screen.

1 For this example, you will need four sticky notes, such as 3M's Post-It notes. On each sheet, draw what is shown below in notes 1, 2, and 3, and the additional 'register' post-it shown in Step 2.

note 1   note 2   note 3

Materials

- sticky notes
- black marker
- tape
- tripod
- video camera
- video tape
- video editing software
- putty (optional)

Registration.
Make sure all the sticky notes are perfectly aligned atop each other. See Chapter 5.1 for more information on registering images.

Anchor the tripod.
Make and place sandbags around the tripod legs to secure your tripod from small bumps.

2 All sticky notes will have to be registered so the notes are perfectly aligned on top of one another (see the registration problem in Chapter 5.1). To do this, securely tape the 'register' sticky note on a flat horizontal surface, table or floor. All other sticky notes will then be placed atop this.

3 Set up the camera and tripod so that the camera is aiming directly at the sticky note. Adjust the zoom and focus on the camera as needed.

4 If you move the camera or accidentally bump it while shooting your scenes, you will have problems with image registering: the camera will be recording from a different angle. To help fix this, mark the tripod's location (e.g., by tape). You can then reposition the camera back to its original location.

RECORDING THE MOVIE

1 You will be recording actions that you want in your movie (e.g., a person pressing a button, as in the first film strip image below), and actions that you will edit out later (e.g., you remove a sticky note to show a different screen, as in the 2nd image below).

After the whole video is recorded, you will use a video editor software to remove the "move screen" sections, shown below crossed with an 'x'. Then replace the edited part with a fade or dissolve transition in between.

2 Place each sticky note on top of the 'register' sticky in the order that you expect to use them. Practice the actions you are going to do.

3 Now press record and leave it on until the whole interaction is complete. The film strip image below shows the order of sequence in which the interaction occurs, as well as what should be deleted. Edit out those segments. You are done!

Sticky putty can be used to keep the bottom of the notes intact.

VARIATIONS: PAPER AND TRANSPARENCY

We can use a variation of this sketching technique to create a video sequence showing a person interacting with a screen where only the appearance of some of its graphical elements changes. Our next example uses paper instead of sticky notes (because the screen is larger) and transparencies. To illustrate, we sketch an interface where a person uses checkboxes to interactively view different colors of a chair she is thinking of buying and to see the cost of that particular item.

Using a similar technique you just learned, prepare the interface shown in step 1. You will need only a single piece of paper showing the basic interface. There are two ways to prepare and create the rest of this video:

Our **first way** pre-makes all the transparencies before you start recording.

1 Draw on one single piece of paper showing the basic interface.

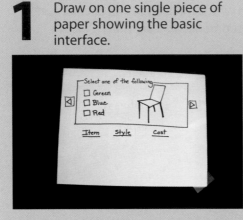

2 Place a transparency atop.

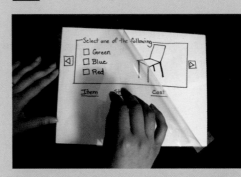

3 On the transparency, draw the changes that would occur after an interaction. In this example, draw in the X in the Blue checkbox, color in the chair, and add "Chair" under Item, "Blue" under Style, and "98.00" under Cost.

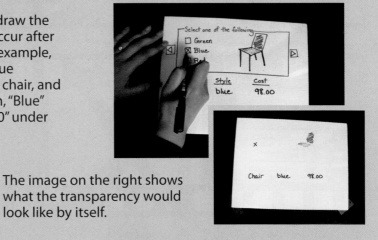

The image on the right shows what the transparency would look like by itself.

Our **second way** places multiple blank transparencies atop the first screen, after which you start recording. This approach allows you to draw while recording. Once you are done with one drawing, the transparency can be lifted off, leaving another blank transparency underneath.

The film strip images below show the sequence of interaction to be recorded. When you edit out your drawing actions (and by replacing it with a dissolve), it will give the illusion that the interface changed as a person did his action.

Tips

For a better interactive effect, have the actor press the checkbox, and then have the actor 'freeze' in that position. Notice in the two deleted scenes that the finger is still in the same place before, during and after the scene change.

Screen 1 – The basic interface

Interaction 1 – The actor presses the Blue checkbox

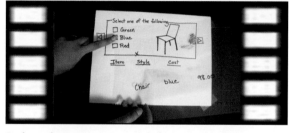

Deleted scene using the first way – slip the pre-made transparency atop the paper interface and beneath the finger.

Final Screen

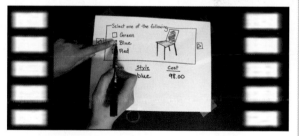

Deleted scene using the second way – with a blank transparency already on top, draw atop the transparency as best you can.

YOU NOW KNOW

You can rapidly create a video of an interaction sequence using conventional video gear, video editing software, and sketches built from off-the-shelf office supplies.

Section 6
Involving Others

Animations provide a visual narrative by playing back a story, or by illustrating different branches in a story. Another use of sequences involves the 'end user' as an actor in the visual narrative, where he has the illusion that his actions affect the underlying dialog. That is, the actor is living the user experience. You can then ask him about his reactions. Alternately, you can show people your work, and ask them to critique it.

6.1 **Uncovering the Initial Mental Model** lets you discover how people initially understand (or don't understand) your sketched interface from its visuals

6.2 **Wizard of Oz** has a human 'wizard' control how your sketch behaves in response to a person's interactions

6.3 **Think Aloud** lets you track what people are thinking by having them tell you what they are doing as they perform tasks on your sketched system

6.4 **Sketch Boards** brings your sketches into the public place, where others can view, discuss, review, and generate ideas around them

6.5 **The Review** outlines several review processes ranging from the informal to the formal, where you can get others to react to your designs

When people see your system for the first time, they will immediately start forming a **mental model** from its visuals: what your system is for, what it lets them do, and how to operate it. This initial model influences how they use and explore the system. As they use the system over time, they will (hopefully) correct any misconceptions they had, and 'fill in the blanks' for the parts of the system they either did not fully understand or did not know about.

This initial mental model is important. An incorrect initial mental model leads to almost immediate frustration, errors and inefficiencies. Because incorrect understandings linger (perhaps for a considerable time), they interfere with ongoing learning and use. They may also cause people to abandon your system, especially in cases where system use is discretionary. This is why it is so important to ensure that your design portrays a good mental model.

Fortunately, you can uncover this initial mental model in the very early stages of design – even in the sketching stage. The method is quite simple. After briefly introducing your design, just ask people to explain, in detail, their understanding of every visual element on the screen. If their explanation doesn't match your intention, then you have spotted a problem in people's mental model that you should try to fix in a redesign.

Case Study: Usability of a Fax Machine

The Situation. I once had problems using an unfamiliar fax machine to send a time-critcial document. Even though I was doing the most basic task expected of a fax machine (to send a fax), I was unsure of its operation, or if the fax was actually sent. Frustrations piled onto frustrations. Afterward, I decided to use this fax machine as a case study for teaching various usability testing methods. Using PowerPoint, I sketched the front panel of the fax machine, which appears on the next page. Back in the classroom, I projected this sketch onto a large display. I then asked for a participant volunteer – a student who had occasional need of a fax machine – to help uncover problems with this system.

The sequence that follows uses this sketched fax machine to illustrate how you can uncover a person's initial mental model. Later chapters will also use this fax machine to illustrate other methods.

Materials

- your sketch

- a test user

Optional:

- video camera and tripod

- another person to take notes of what happens

Paper Feed Tray

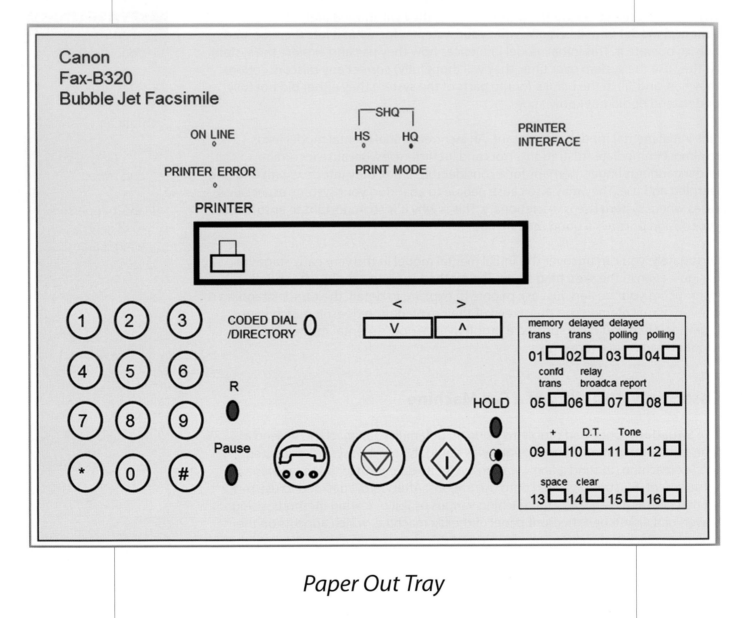

Paper Out Tray

UNCOVERING THE MENTAL MODEL

1 Preparing for Data Collecting

You need to set up the room and your materials so you can record what happens. Ideally, you should set up a video camera pointing at the person and the sketch so you can record the session for later review. Alternately, you could have another person present whose job is just to observe and take notes. You could try to take notes about what you see, but there is usually just too much going on (and at too fast a pace) for you to both give instructions and record activities in real time.

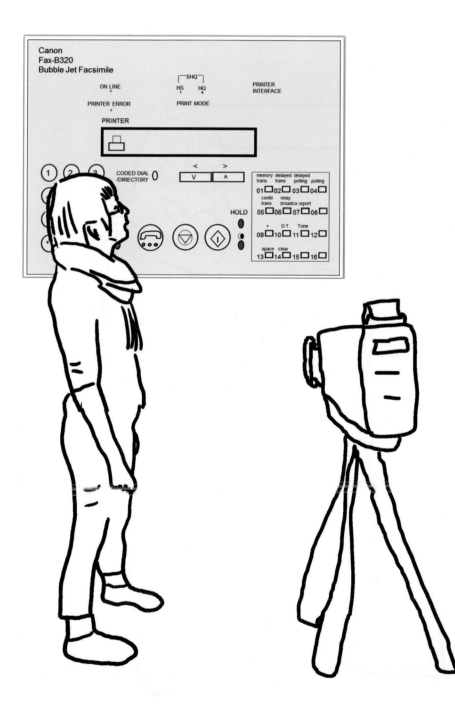

2 **Introducing the Method**

You need to tell the person what you are going to ask him to do. You also need to be very clear that you are looking for any problems he may have doing some of the things you are going ask him to do. Gommol and Nicol (1990) suggest the following dialogue as a standard opener to a test involving users.

3

Introducing the System

You need to introduce the system to set the context. That is, give your participant just enough information to help him get into the right frame of mind. You may want to add information about the interface that is not apparent in the sketch, but would be apparent in the final system. Avoid disclosing information or hints about the actual system operation, as this would unduly influence how the person forms his initial mental model.

For example:

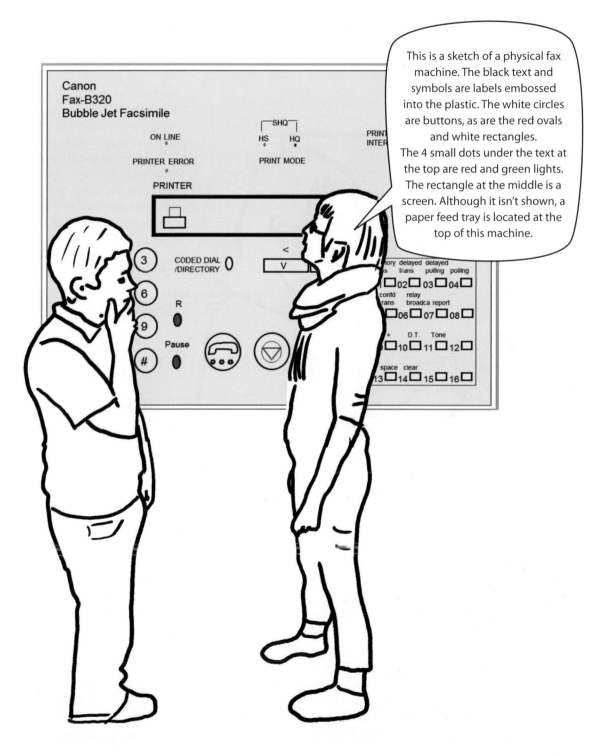

4 **Marching Orders**
Now tell your participant what you want him to do and how to do it.

> Starting from the top left corner, tell me what you think everything means – the labels, the clusters of controls, individual buttons, everything. Point to the things you are describing. Tell me what you are certain about, where you are just guessing, or where you haven't a clue. If you miss anything, I may ask you to go back and explain it.

Exercise

Before reading on, try the above exercise yourself. That is, walk through the interface and note down what you are certain about, where you are just guessing, or where you haven't a clue.

The caveat is that 'trying it yourself' wouldn't work if you were the actual system designer, as designers already have a mental model of the system. The reason why designers use test users is to see whether the users' mental model as acquired by the visuals matches the designer's intended mental model.

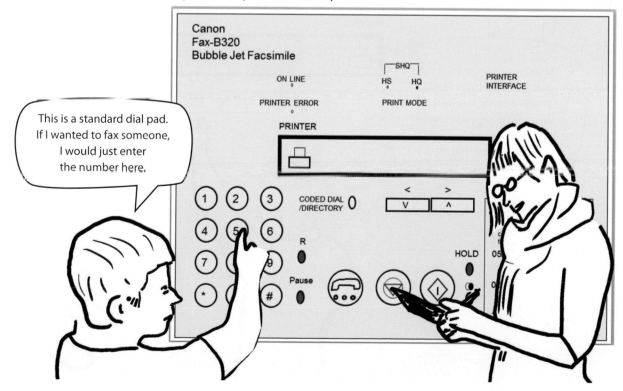

5 **The Participant's Model**
A sampling of typical things that a person may say is illustrated here. The first segment shows the person explaining the labels. Note how the 'experimenter' is taking notes.

Somewhat later, the person explains the dial pad...

…and then the large icons…

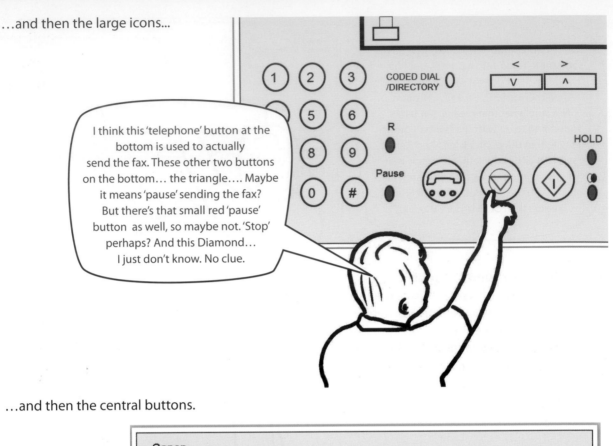

…and then the central buttons.

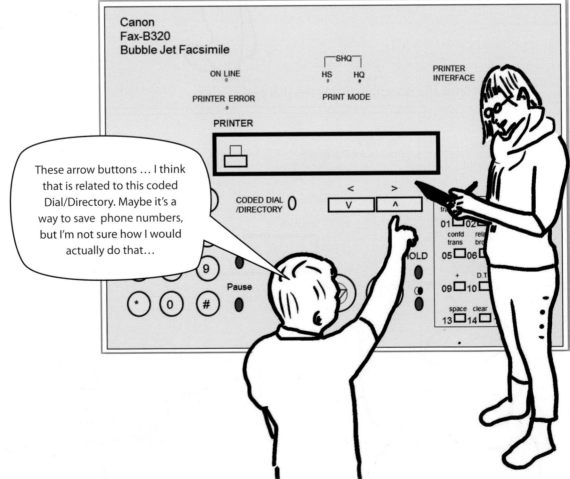

The description above is only part of what the participant would say. In actual tests we did with people, almost all of them were quite confused about the cluster of buttons on the right, where at best they made wild (and usually wrong) guesses about what they did.

Exercise

Before reading on, try the above exercise with a test user. Have him walk through the entire visuals: it should take between 5–10 minutes. Take notes. From those notes, try to identify particular problems or classes of problems. Then redo the design to fix these problems. To make it 'real', try to keep to the constraints of the existing fax machine, where your new design could be done at little or no extra cost. Our solution is detailed below and on the next page.

Tip

While we explained how the above process can be used to uncover someone's initial mental model, it also works to uncover that person's mental model after a period of use. This can reveal persistent misconceptions a person may have about the system, as well as holes in his or her knowledge.

6 Identifying Problems Through the Mental Model

Even the brief fragment above tells us a lot. While we saw that people quickly recognized the dial pad as a way to enter phone numbers, that is about it for the good news. Considerable problems are revealed with this sketch design, where people were unable to form an accurate mental model of it. For example, the meaning of the labels are cryptic, in part because people did not know the meaning of the abbreviations (e.g., 'HQ' actually stands for 'High Quality'), and because it is not in their own language (e.g., what does 'PRINTER INTERFACE' really mean?). They were unsure about the primary buttons at the bottom that triggered dialing the number and sending (or cancelling) the fax. The central buttons are similarly cryptic. Even if people guessed at the correct function of some controls (such as the arrow buttons to save numbers), they could not say how they would actually go about using them (e.g., the actual sequence of operations necessary to save a number). And some controls are just plain mysterious, such as the cluster at the right.

7 Iterating the Design to Solve These Problems

Our next step is to redo the sketch to 'fix' some of these problems. Consider our solution on the next page. We redid the labeling: we removed all abbreviations, we rewrote them in the user's language, and we added labels to the large button icons. We spatially and visually grouped related controls together (the phone directory, the printing boxes, the dial/send buttons and the pause/cancel buttons). We put a plastic cover over the cryptic panel on the right, which visually tells the person that these controls are not needed for basic tasks but are available for advanced uses. Finally, we moved a few things unnecessary to the basic operation into this advanced control panel, e.g., the 'hold' buttons. The total cost of this improvement is minimal (the plastic cover adds costs, but removing some of the buttons saves costs). This is not to say that this design is perfect – it isn't. However, it's probably better than the previous version. And we can test it again – remember, our previous test only took about 10 minutes to do!

Note

The sequence illustrated here is an example of the Narrative storyboard method introduced in Chapter 4.4.

It didn't take long to do. We used PowerPoint to create the fax machine (Chapter 3.6), and photo-traces to capture three poses each of two people (Chapter 3.9).

We made our narrative visually dynamic simply by altering the cropping of the scene, and by changing the size and position of the photo-traced people within it.

We also horizontally flipped the photo-trace of a person. This let us reuse a pose while still making it look somewhat different across panels.

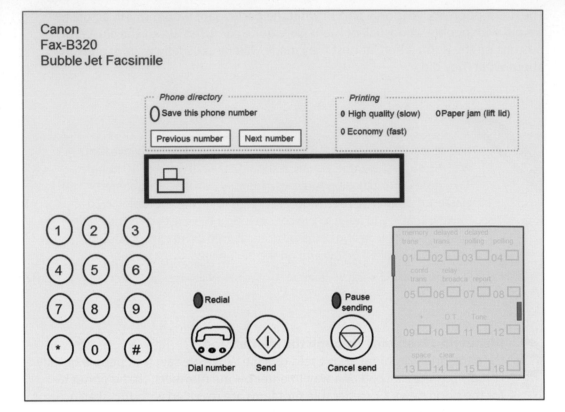

Exercise

Repeat the above process with one of your own sketches, or an unfamiliar application, or even a web site (try a travel web site or an airline site). Do this more than once. What is important is that you get familiar with this process, and that you discover how many problems (and successes) you can uncover in a short amount of time by looking for mismatches between your participant's initial mental model and your own model of what the system design was supposed to do.

References

Nicol, A. and Gomoll, K. (1990) *User Observation: Guidelines for Apple Developers.* Apple Human Interface Notes #1, January 1990.

YOU NOW KNOW

Your visuals tell a story about your system, and people will form an initial mental model of how your system works from it. You can quickly uncover this model simply by asking them to explain the visuals. By looking for mismatches and gaps between their model and how the system is actually supposed to work, you can identify problems that you can repair in your next design iteration.

Most of the interactions seen so far are fairly simple state transition diagrams. We've also shown how prospective 'users' can actually drive the animation of such systems by actions, giving the illusion that the system actually exists. Yet this only works when we know what user action will lead from one state to another. There are two situations where this next step cannot be anticipated easily.

1. **Difficulty of understanding input.** Unlike a simple button press or menu selection, your animated sketch may not be able to understand the user's input action, e.g., gestures, speech, or the meaning of entered text.

2. **Responding to input.** The response of your animated sketch depends on the user's action and thus cannot be anticipated, e.g., the actual text entered.

The problem is that your animated sketch has no real back-end to understand and to respond to complex input. The solution is to make a human – a **Wizard** – the back-end. We'll illustrate how this works by examples that people have actually used to examine futuristic system ideas.

EXAMPLE 1: THE LISTENING TYPEWRITER

In 1984, senior executives did not normally use computers. The issue was that they saw typing as something that secretaries did. To solve this problem, John Gould and his colleagues at IBM wanted to develop a 'listening typewriter', where executives would dictate to the computer, using speech to compose and edit letters, memos, and documents. While such speech recognition systems are now commonly available, at that time Gould didn't know if such systems would actually be useful or if it would be worth IBM's high development cost. He decided to prototype a listening typewriter using **Wizard of Oz**. He also wanted to look at two conditions: a system that could understand isolated words spoken one at a time (i.e., with pauses between words), and a continuous speech recognition system. Our example will illustrate the isolated words condition.

Note

The Wizard of Oz method is named after the well-known 1939 movie of the same name. The Wizard is an intimidating being who appears as a large disembodied face surrounded by smoke and flames and who speaks in a booming voice. However, Toto the dog exposes the Wizard as a fake when he pulls away a curtain to reveal a very ordinary man operating a console that controls the appearance and sound of the Wizard.

Around 1980, John Kelley adapted the 'Wizard of Oz' term to experimental design, where he acted as the 'man behind the curtain' to simulate a computer's response to people's natural language commands.

John Gould and others popularized the idea in 1984 through his listening typewriter study, as detailed in Example 1.

What the User Saw

The sketch below shows what the user – an executive – would see. The user would speak individual words into the microphone, where the spoken words (if known by the computer) would appear as text on the screen. If the computer did not know the word, a series of XXXXs would appear. The user would also have the opportunity to correct errors by special commands. For example, if the user said 'NUTS' the computer would erase the last word, while NUTS 5 would erase the last 5 words. Other special words let the user tell the computer to spell out unknown words (via 'SPELLMODE' and 'ENDSPELLMODE', and add formatting (e.g., 'CAPIT' to capitalize the first letter of a word, and 'NEWPARAGRAPH' for a new paragraph).

What Was Actually Happening

Computers at that time could not do this kind of speech recognition reliably, so Gould and colleagues simulated it. They used a combination of a human Wizard that interpreted what the user said, and a computer that had simple rules for what to do with words typed to it by the Wizard. The sketch below shows how this was done. The Wizard typist, located in a different room, listened to each word the user said, and then typed that word into the computer. The computer would then check each word typed to see if it was in its limited dictionary. If it was, it would display it on the user's screen. If it wasn't it would display XXXXs. For special command words, the typist would enter an abbreviation of it, which the computer would interpret as a command to trigger the desired effect on the user's screen.

Tip

The Designer benefits by becoming the Wizard due to the "training" received by playing the role of Wizard. Being personally responsible for a person's discomfort and confusion motivates revisions! And simulating an incomplete design reveals its ill-defined aspects.

Keeping It Real

The chief danger in using a Wizard of Oz is that the Wizard can have powers of comprehension that no system could have. For example, a human Wizard can understand complex speech or gestural input that cannot be implemented reliably. The solution – as done in the listening typewriter – is to limit the Wizard's intelligence to things that can be implemented realistically (see the 1993 paper by Maulsby, Greenberg, and Mander for more details and another example of how this can be done).

1. **The Wizard's understanding of user input is based on a constrained input interaction model** that explicitly lists the kinds of instructions that a system – if implemented – can understand and the feedback it can formulate. For example, even though the typist could understand and type continuous speech, the typist was told to listen to just a single spoken word, type in that spoken word, and then hit <enter>. The typist was also told to recognize and translate certain words as commands, which were then entered as an abbreviation. The computer further constrained input by recognizing only those words and commands in its limited vocabulary.

2. **The Wizard's response should be based on an 'algorithm' or 'rules'** that limits the actions it takes to those that can be realistically implemented at a later time. For example, if the user said "type 10 exclamation marks", the Wizard's algorithm would be to just type in that phrase exactly, rather than '!!!!!'. Similarly, the computer substituted XXXXs for words it could not understand, and could respond to only a small set of editing commands.

EXAMPLE 2: ROBOTIC INTERRUPTION

In their 2011 paper, Paul Saulnier and his colleagues wanted to see how a person would respond to a robot that interrupted him, where the robot's behavior depended on the urgency of the situation. They were interested in how simple robot actions are interpreted by a person. This includes: how the robot moves toward and looks at a person seated in an office, whether the robot does this from outside or at the doorway, how close the robot approaches, and its speed of motion. Yet to build such a robot would be difficult, as the robot would have to know how to locate the person and move toward him, all while doing appropriate physical behaviors. Instead, they simulated the robot's behavior by Wizard of Oz.

What the Person Saw

The person, who was seated in a room near a doorway, would see the robot move outside the doorway. In one condition, the person would see the robot slowly come to the doorway, glance in at him for several seconds, and then leave. In another condition, the person would see the robot enter the room doorway, gaze directly at him, (as seen in the figure below) and even rotate its head back and forth to try to give the person a sense of urgency.

What Was Actually Happening

As with the Listening Typewriter, a Wizard, sitting out of sight just outside the doorway, was actually remotely controlling the robot. Unlike the Listening Typewriter, the person knew that the Wizard was there. The Wizard controlled the robot using a gamepad controller to issue commands, which in turn would control the robot's direction and speed, and buttons corresponding to short pre-programmed sequences of robot behavior (e.g., head shaking).

EXAMPLE 3: THE FAX MACHINE

As a teaching exercise, I (author Greenberg) used Wizard of Oz to illustrate how even a very simple sketch could be used to test an interface. In the previous chapter, I described how I created a sketch of a fax machine, projected that sketch onto a wall, and then invited a student to explain it so I could determine his initial mental model. We continue from there. I told the student that the feed tray was at the bottom of the fax, and then handed the student a sheet of paper and said, "Send this document to our main office, whose fax number is 666-9548. As you do so, tell me what you are doing and thinking." This method, called **think aloud**, will be discussed in detail in Chapter 6.3.

Typically, a student would start by touching the numbers on the dial pad on the projected screen and say something like what is shown in the first image: "I enter the number 666-9546 on this keypad…" as he did each key press. The problem is that the "fax machine" was just a single sketched image, so it could not respond to his actions. To fix this problem, I become the Wizard, where I would tell the student how the fax machine would respond, for example "666-9548 appears on the little display."

I even simulated noises, such as the modem sound that occurs when the person presses the "send" button at the bottom, as shown in the second image.

This example differs considerably from the previous ones in that the system "responses" are not actually done on the sketch, but occur in the imagination of the students as they listen to the Wizard's description. Yet in spite of this, students bought into this easily. As students tried to do more complex tasks (such as "store your number so you can redial it later"), they were clearly exploring the interface of the fax machine and its responses (as told to them by the Wizard) to try to learn how to complete their task. They became immersed in the "system" as sketch.

This example also shows why it is important for the Wizard to understand the algorithm – in this case the responses of the fax machine – to a user's input. The Wizard needed to know what each button press would do. In difficult tasks, such as the number storing one, the Wizard had to know the 'correct' sequence of events to store a number. The Wizard also had to know what would happen if the user got things wrong, where the user would press other incorrect buttons and button sequences during an attempt to solve the task.

Note

Does the Wizard have to be the "man behind the curtain"? The three examples differ considerably in the relationship between the Wizard and the participant. The participant in the Listening Typewriter was 'deceived' into thinking the system was real, as he was completely unaware of the Wizard. In Robotic Interruption, the participant was introduced to the Wizard and told that the Wizard was operating the robot, but the Wizard was kept out of view during the actual simulation. In the Fax Machine, the participant was very aware of the Wizard, as not only was the Wizard next to him but was telling him what the response would be as part of their conversation. No system feedback was provided by the sketch itself.

Yet in all cases, people usually buy into the simulation. We suspect that in routine Wizard of Oz simulations, the degree to which you have to hide the presence of the Wizard won't be critical. Of course, there will be always exceptions to this rule that depend on the situation.

References

Gould, J.D., Conti, J., and Hovanyecz, T. (1983) *Composing Letters with a Simulated Listening Typewriter.* Communications of the ACM 26, 4 (April), pp. 295–308.

Kelley, J.F. (1984) *An Iterative Design Methodology for User-Friendly Natural Language Office Information Applications.* ACM Transactions on Office Information Systems, March, 2:1, pp. 26–41.

Maulsby, D., Greenberg, S., and Mander, R. (1993) *Prototyping an intelligent agent through Wizard of Oz.* Proceedings of the ACM CHI'93 Conference on Human Factors in Computing Systems, Amsterdam, The Netherlands, ACM Press, pp. 277–284.

Saulnier, P., Sharlin, E., and Greenberg, S. (2011) E*xploring Minimal Nonverbal Interruption in HRI.* Proceedings of the IEEE International Symposium on Robot and Human Interactive Communication (Ro-Man 2011), Atlanta, Georgia, IEEE Press.

YOU NOW KNOW

You can act as the 'back-end' of your system, where you act as a Wizard that interprets people's input actions and where you trigger (or perform) the expected system response. To keep this real, you need to constrain your interpretations and responses to those that your sketched system could actually perform.

I'm navigating the web site of this store...

Chapter 6.1 showed how you can uncover a person's initial mental model formed when he or she sees your sketched system for the first time. Yet that technique does not reveal how that person's view of your system unfolds as he or she actually tries to use it.

Passive observation is one simple but not particularly effective method. The idea is that you introduce the sketched system to a person, and then you observe how that person uses it. Observation lets you see the person's physical acts. From these, you can perhaps infer what is going on. Hesitations suggest difficulties. Successful quick actions suggest no problems. Incorrect actions suggest mis-understanding and errors. However, your inferences will be superficial, as you will never really know what is going on in a person's head.

This is where the **think aloud method** helps. As briefly introduced in Chapter 6.2, the approach is to have people think aloud, where they say what they are thinking as they use your sketch to do a task. This method is easy to learn, cheap, simple and fast to do. Yet it can reveal a significant amount of information, especially usability problems. As Gomoll and Nicol [1990] explain,

> "by listening to participants think and plan, you can examine their expectations for your product, as well as their intentions and their problem solving strategies."

Catching and repairing usability and conceptual problems during the early design phase can lead to significant savings in the development process. These and other reasons explain why think aloud is the most frequently used evaluation method employed by professional user experience designers and usability engineers.

STEPS OF THINK ALOUD

There are many books that describe the think-aloud method and its variations. Some go into great detail, as in Dumais and Redish's *Practical Guide to Usability Testing*. Books like these should be required reading if you are taking usability testing seriously, as they go into excellent detail about how to set up studies, how to define tasks, how to prepare for the test, ethics in running a test, and so on.

However, a few simple steps can get you going right away. Perhaps the shortest and best summary of think aloud was produced by Gomoll and Nicol in their 1999 paper: ***User Observation: Guidelines for Apple Developers***. This chapter reproduces liberally from these guidelines, albeit (with apologies to them) in a somewhat pictorial, modified and summarized form.

Materials

- task description

- sketches to match the task flow

- video recording equipment to capture user actions and talk

- one or more test users

Preparation

a. **Set an objective.** Take time to figure out what you're testing and what you're not. In other words, determine an objective that focuses on a specific aspect of the product. By limiting the scope of the test, you're more likely to get information that helps you solve a specific problem.

b. **Design the tasks.** You should give your participant one or more specific tasks to do. These tasks should be real tasks that you expect most users will do when they use your product. After you determine which tasks to use, write them out as short, simple instructions.

c. **Prepare your sketch so that people can interact with it.** If you want to explore how people do particular tasks, make sure that the expected interaction sequences are available (e.g., as in a scripted slide show, described in Chapter 4.1). When a person does an action, you can then manually switch the sketch to the next scene. Alternately, use a branching storyboard (Chapter 4.3) to have the system give the illusion that it is actually responding to them. Or you can reveal system responses via Wizard of Oz (Chapter 6.2). Your sketch doesn't need to cover everything; your on-going instructions can limit the scope of what your test user should be trying to do.

d. **Prepare equipment.** If you are audio or video-recording the session, make sure it's set up ahead of time and working well.

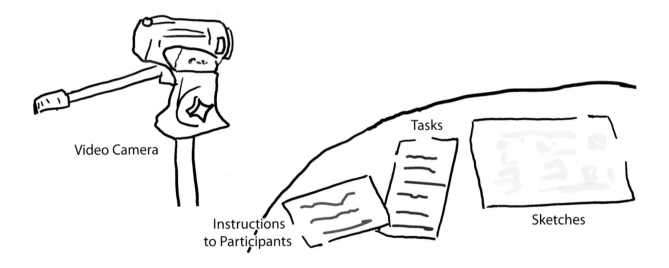

Video Camera

Instructions to Participants

Tasks

Sketches

2 The Test

A. Introduce yourself, and describe the purpose of the observation (in general terms). Set the participant at ease by stressing that you're trying to find problems in the product. For example:

> Hi, I'm Joe. You're helping us by trying out this product in its early stages. We're looking for places where the product may be difficult to use. If you have trouble with some of the tasks, it's the product's fault, not yours. Don't feel bad; that's exactly what we're looking for. If we can locate the trouble spots, then we can go back and improve the product. Remember, we're testing the product, not you.

B. Tell the participant that it's okay to quit at any time. Participants shouldn't fell like they're locked into completing tasks.

> Although I don't know of any reason for this to happen, if you should become uncomfortable or find this test objectionable in any way, you are free to quit at any time.

> I'm going to use this video camera to record what you are doing and saying. As you can see, the camera will only be pointing at the sketch and your hands, not your face. I'll use this video to review our session later for things I may have missed. No one else but me will ever see this video. Are you ok with that?

C. Talk about the equipment in the room. Explain the purpose of each piece of equipment (hardware, software, video camera, microphones, etc.), how it is used in the test, and what you will do with any collected data.

D. Explain how to think aloud. For example:

We have found that we get a great deal of information from these informal tests if we ask people to think aloud as they work through the exercises. It may be a bit awkward at first, but it's really very easy once you get used to it. All you do is speak your thoughts as you work. If you forget to think aloud, I'll remind you to keep talking. Would you like me to demonstrate?

E. Explain that you cannot provide help. Participants should work with your product without any interference or extra help, as it will reveal how they would really interact with the product. The exception is when you see a problem that may stop them from going on, or that leads to excessive frustration. In that case (and perhaps after a bit of time has passed) you can step in and give them a hint. This will let them continue, where you can uncover problems later in the task sequence.

As you're working through the exercises, I won't be able to provide help or answer questions. This is because we want to create the most realistic situation possible. Even though I won't be able to answer your questions, please ask them anyway. It's very important that I capture all your questions and comments for our record. When you've finished all the exercises, I'll answer any questions you still have.

F. Describe the tasks and introduce the product. Explain what the participant should do and in what order. Explain that because he is working over a sketch, that you may be able to simulate only a few of the system's responses.

G. Ask if there are any questions before you start. Then begin the observation.

Ok, you asked me to visit the home page of this on-line store, and try to buy a shirt over it. So I'm looking for something like 'start shopping'. Hmm. I can't find it. But there is this button called directories. Maybe it's under that? No, that's not it – it is a bunch of phone numbers. Ok, how do I get back to the main screen? I'll click the store icon. Oops, that's not the page I saw before; it looks like the corporate headquarters page, not the shopping page. Ugggh. I'm not sure what to do next…

H. If the participant stops talking, remind him.

<Stops talking…>

… What are you thinking? What are you trying to do? Can you tell me what you are looking for?

I. Conclude the observation. When the test is over, explain what you were trying to find out during the test, answer any remaining questions the participant may have, discuss any interesting behaviors you would like the participant to explain. This could include the participant's own thoughts about where things went wrong and possible design suggestions.

USE THE RESULTS

As you observe, you see users doing things you never expect them to do. If you see a participant struggling or making mistakes, you should attribute the difficulties to faulty product design, not to the participant. To get the most out of your test results, review all your data carefully and thoroughly (as captured in your notes and the video). Look for places where participants had trouble, and see if you can determine how your design could be changed to alleviate the problems. Look for patterns in the participants' behavior that might tell you whether the product was understood correctly.

1. Getting Warmed Up

To get you 'in the groove', try a think-aloud test using an existing software system. A web page to (say) an airline site would be an excellent example. Create a few tasks, starting from a simple one to increasingly complex ones. For example:

a. Find a flight that goes from here to Los Angeles, leaving tomorrow.

b. Find the cheapest flight that goes between these two cities, where you would prefer to leave late in the day but come back first thing in the morning a week later.

c. Find an itinerary that goes from here to London, stops in London for two days, then continues on to New Delhi, and then returns here a week after that.

2. Using the Fax Machine Sketch

Using the fax machine sketch from Chapter 6.1, do a usability test of it. For example:

a. Here is a 1-page fax. Send it to 222-3333.

b. You think the fax machine can save phone numbers so you can recall them later. Save the number 222-3333 to the fax machine. Once you've done that, recall it and send that fax to it again.

Note that you may have trouble with the above, as you don't know how this particular fax machine works and thus can't really simulate what will happen using Wizard of Oz. But try it anyway – you will still learn a lot about where people will stumble.

3. Using Your Own Sketch

Once you've tried this, take a sketch you developed, create several tasks for it (going from the most basic to something a bit more complex), and run a test on it.

References

Nicol, A. and Gomoll, K. (1990) *User Observation: Guidelines for Apple Developers*. Apple Human Interface Notes #1, January 1990.

Dumais, J.S. and Redish, J.C. (1999) *A Practical Guide to Usability Testing*. Revised Edition. Intellect Books.

YOU NOW KNOW

Think aloud reveals what people are thinking as they try out your sketch. It is one of the most frequently used usability test methods, is cheap, fast to do, and produces a rich amount of information.

Once you have created a set of sketches for a particular project, you should take every opportunity to present them to and share them with others. Telling others stories about your sketches will clarify your thinking about them. Questions people ask (and your answers to them) will often reveal new insights. Overall, suggestions and critique by others will lead to inspiration, uncover problems you have not yet considered, and introduce new ideas.

This chapter shows how to prepare and structure sketch boards and several ways to share them with others.

PREPARATION METHOD 1: FOAM CORE POSTER SHEETS

1 **Select a Canvas: Foam Core Boards**
You need a large empty "canvas" to arrange your sketches into a *sketch board*. To make your sketch boards portable, you can use large foam core sheets to put your sketches on. Using these sheets makes it easier for you to take them to any location where you would like to discuss them.

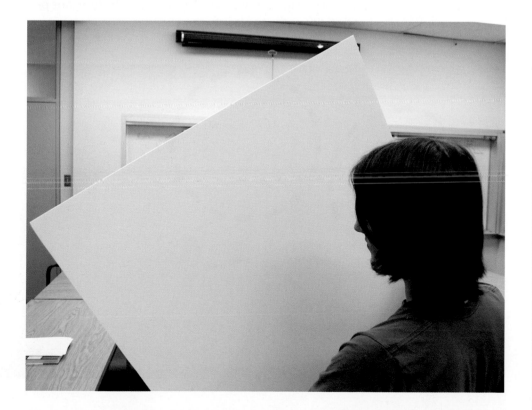

Materials

- foam core poster sheets (cost around $7–$15 in office supply or hobby stores)

- pins or tape

- sticky notes

- paper for sketches (and/or photo copies from your sketchbook)

- pens (medium pen tip for sketches, thicker wide tip for headlines)

Tip

Keep Originals
If you re-use sketches from your sketchbook, take photo copies so the originals stay in the book.

Flexibility
You can use pins instead of tape to fix your sketches to the poster sheets. This makes it easier to rearrange your sketches later.

Alternatives
Often there are multiple ways to structure, cluster, and classify your sketches. Take photos of the sketch board whenever you try out an alternative layout of the sketches. This way you can easily compare them afterwards.

2 **Arrange Your Sketches**
Arrange all relevant sketches on the poster sheet.

3 **Restructure and Categorize**
The spatial layout of sketches on the poster boards helps to structure the sketches. When the sketches belong to similar themes, you may want to group them into clusters. For example, in this photo the sketches have been rearranged into four clusters according to the most important project goals. We also used sticky notes to classify the clusters.

PREPARATION METHOD 2: STICKY NOTES AND WHITEBOARDS

1 **Arrange Sticky Note Sketches on Whiteboard**
If you don't need portable sketch boards, you can put your sketches onto a whiteboard or wall. If you sketch using sticky notes, you can later stick them directly onto the whiteboard. For example, the photo below illustrates a person putting up several sketched storyboard sequences onto a whiteboard. He uses different paper colors (blue, orange, white) as clear indicators to which sequence a sketch belongs.

2 **Rearranging and Sorting**
Again, you can rearrange and sort your sketches once they are up on the board. Using the sticky notes makes rearranging your sketches even easier. This is particularly useful for sketches illustrating a time sequence such as storyboards.

SHARE YOUR SKETCHES WITH OTHERS

The sketch boards can be a good starting point to trigger discussions about your current project. Here are a few suggestions of where you can share your sketches.

Arrange Them Around Your Desk

You can also put the sketch boards for your current projects around your work desk. The visibility of the sketches can inspire you when glancing at them, and are a good starting point for conversations and discussions when fellow co-workers or passers by meet you in your office.

Since the foam core boards are very light weight, you can easily hang them on any wall using thin wire or double sided tape, or put them on a shelf leaning against the wall. Below you can see the desk of one of the co-authors of this book, surrounded by poster boards with sketches of different ongoing projects.

Discuss Them During Meetings

Bring your sketch boards to meetings where you plan to discuss your projects. You can then refer to particular sketches when explaining the project ideas, and gather feedback about the initial design (also see the chapter of how to organize design critiques).

Place Them in Public Areas

Depending on the project and type of sketches, you might also want to make your idea sketches even more visible to your group or organization. To do so, place your sketch boards in the hallway or any other public area (such as a lounge or a library room) of your group. Gould (1988) calls this "hallway and storefront methodology".

Customer Location

You can place your sketch boards at customer locations (see page 99 of Gould, 1988). This way, you increase the visibility of your early design sketches to the people who will later use your system.

Take a few of your exisiting sketches (e.g., photo copies from your sketchbook) and arrange them on a sketch board. Use at least one of the presented techniques to share this sketch board with others. Note down all of their comments, and use that to prime your next step down the design funnel.

References

Gould, J. D. (1988) *How to design usable systems.* In: Readings in Human-Computer Interaction. R. M. Baecker, J. Grudin, W. A. S. Buxton, S. Greenberg (Eds.). Second Edition, Morgan Kaufmann Publishers, San Francisco, USA.

YOU NOW KNOW

By applying the techniques presented in this chapter you can create sketch boards and gain new insights by structuring and categiorizing your collections of sketches. To increase the visibility of your sketched ideas and to motivate others to provide feedback and suggestions, you can now apply one or more of the presented sharing techniques.

Other chapters in this book repeatedly stated that sketches can be a valuable conversational prop for presenting your ideas to others and for gathering feedback from them in the form of constructive criticism. Presenting ideas and gathering feedback is something you should do constantly in various situations. These can range from brief informal discussions, to scheduled periodic meetings where you present your ideas formally to others and gather structured feedback from them.

Andy Pressman begins his book **Architecture 101** by introducing the design studio, which is immediately followed by a section titled 'Seeking Criticism'. He offers this advice:

> "**Seeking Criticism**. Receiving criticism is a fundamental part of learning in the studio. *Make sure that your work is reviewed and discussed as often as possible.* … Criticism is a fact of professional life. While there is unquestionably some utility in the intense evaluation of the merits and shortcomings of your work, it is never easy to take. Even when you just *know* that there could not be a more elegant solution, incorporation of [the critic's] modifications *almost always translates to an opportunity to make the work even more potent.*" [condensed from Pressman, p. 3]

Remember the design funnel introduced in Chapter 1.2, and the importance of considering alternative solutions and variations as the design progresses? The review is yet another way to probe you into doing this. It is all too easy for you as a designer to get locked into an idea.

It is the role of the critic to push and prod you to constantly reconsider your design. And it is your role to present your work in a way that others can understand (and thus respond to) your ideas, and to track and reflect on the feedback they offer.

1 **You present your work so people – your critics – can understand the key points behind it.** If your presentation is poor, your critics will not be able to respond appropriately. The sketch has a key role to play here, as it is a concrete representation of your idea.

2 **Critics verbally review your work.** They summarize your ideas (which lets you see if they understand what you presented and gives you a chance to correct misconceptions). They say what they consider its strengths. They state its weaknesses and what could be improved. They offer solutions to problems they see and alternatives. They challenge you to think differently.

Materials

- your sketches

- your planned verbal talk explaining your design

- people to talk to

- a place to meet

3 **You gather feedback.** It's critical that you listen to their comments, and you record them (e.g., in your sketchbook). If you don't, the whole process will be a waste of time.

4 **You reflect on this criticism and re-evaluate your ideas.** Consider everything people say, and use that to make your idea even better. Don't be defensive. While you may not agree with them, at the very least you should evaluate each statement they make and make an objective decision on how (and if) you want to apply it.

Reviews come in many forms, and we detail only a few approaches below. We begin with the most informal review (the elevator pitch) and end with the most formal. We highly recommend Parnell and Sara's (2007) book **The Crit**, as it is an excellent and highly accessible handbook of how to prepare and run a critique. Although written for architecture students, almost all of it is applicable to interaction designers. Pressman's (1993) book **Architecture 101** also has some valuable advice.

THE ELEVATOR PITCH

Take every opportunity to tell others about your idea, no matter where you are. You should always be prepared to give someone a very brief summary of your idea, and give him or her time to respond to it. As the name *elevator pitch* implies, this can happen anywhere, and the time you have with the other person can be very short (from 30 seconds to 2 minutes).

Constructing a good elevator pitch is much harder to do than it sounds. You can't assume that your audience knows anything about your idea or its background. This begs the question: How do we construct an elevator pitch? The best answer is by Bruce Macdonald (University of Auckland), who said the following about effective presentations:

> "I can't overemphasize the importance of being clear in your own mind of what you want the audience to get from your presentation. Only then can you really concentrate on doing a good job of getting it across."

The key is: *know your message.* Distilling your idea (including the problem you are trying to solve) into a 30-second statement means that *you have to know exactly what your main idea is*, and then present it clearly. Everything you say (and what you decide to leave out) is built around this message. Your sketchbook (which you will be carrying with you, of course!) can help, where you have deliberately constructed a sketch that will help you illustrate this main idea during your 30 seconds.

Some things you may want to include in an elevator pitch are:

* *Who you are and your role.*

* *The problem you are working on and the motivation behind it.*

* *Your design idea. [A storyboard in the sketchbook can illustrate this].*

* *Invitations for feedback.*

This example contains all the above points (121 words, and ~30 – 60 seconds to say it over a sketch):

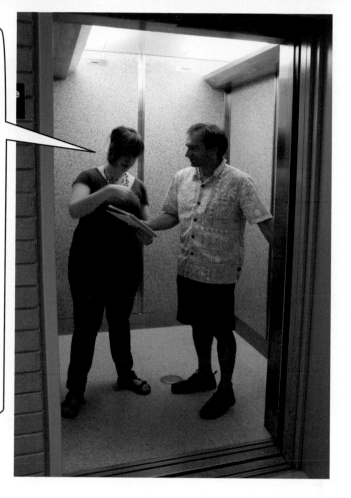

I design interactive web browsers for Smart Phones.

The problem is that when people want to search the web, they often have trouble typing text on their phone's browser, especially if they are on the move.

My solution is to have people speak single words into the phone, where they will see that word added to the browser's search box.

Shows a storyboard in the sketchbook is used to illustrate this sequence].

If the phone's understanding is wrong, they just try again, and the new search term is displayed.

I'd love to hear about what you like or dislike about this idea, and how you think it could be improved.

THE DESKTOP REVIEW

If you work in a public environment such as a studio, you should always be prepared to present and invite critique of your work as it progresses. This can include the colleagues who sit nearby, senior mentors who track your progress and offer periodic advice, managers who walk by occasionally, visitors to your studio, and even clients who drop in.

We already introduced Sketch Boards in Chapter 6.4 as a method that can help you make this happen. However, other methods introduced in this book also work. This can include using key drawings in your sketchbook, a PowerPoint presentation readily available on your computer, a video or other animation that you can play at any time, a mocked up physical prototype, a scripted slide show that you can have people try, and so on.

As mentioned in Chapter 6.4, the key point is to have sketches on display so they invite discussion and feedback. This includes a physical sketch as a teaser, where you can start the discussion with an elevator pitch. If people are interested, you can then go into greater detail about your work as revealed in other sketches that you may not have on public display (e.g., those on your computer), where you discuss its nuances with them. This means you should also have detailed sketches readily available to pull out at a moment's notice.

You should also keep a special pad permanently on your desk to capture people's comments, as it's all too easy to forget what they say. Take it out as soon as people are there.

THE MEETING

You will likely want to arrange meetings with colleagues and mentors at opportune times, where you explicitly seek feedback as your ideas evolve.

The challenge is that you may have attendees who are not designers: you may need to 'teach' them how to give you good feedback. An untrained attendee may not say anything, or may limit feedback to only positive points as he or she doesn't want to make you feel bad, or (on the other extreme) aggressively attack your work.

There are 'tricks' you can use to train your audience.

1 **Give them some context to what you are looking for.**
Tell them that you are presenting your work because you need feedback about it. Stress that while they should say what is good, you will likely get more value from them if: they expose weak ideas; they state what could be improved; they recommend how to improve it; they offer design alternatives.

2 **Have them take turns saying what they like and what could be improved.**
If your audience is larger than just a few people, go "round robin" around the room. Alternate what each person does, where the first person states a single thing they like about your idea, while the second person states what can be improved (and ideally offers ideas on how to improve it). Give people the opportunity to 'pass' if they can't think of anything. Then go around the room again where people switch roles.

3 **Don't defend or discuss your work as people are giving you feedback.**
Listen to what people say, and write it down. At most, paraphrase what they have said back to them to make sure you understand the point they have made. This will give the audience more time to state and embellish their opinions.

4 **Open up a discussion.**
After people have exhausted what they want to say to you, you can open up discussion around the key points they made that you wish to explore further. You may want to clarify some things about your work, but as mentioned before, you shouldn't defend it. Your job is to get them to clarify the problems raised, and to discuss solutions and design alternatives to these problems as a group.

THE FORMAL REVIEW (OR THE CRIT)

There will be times where you will have to formally present your work to others. This could arise from:

- **Scheduled checkpoints** during your project, where you show your progress to others on your team, to your managers and supervisors, and possibly to clients.

- **Delivery of your project,** where you show your 'final' work to others. If a student, this could be part of your defense. If a professional, this could be part of the decision process to 'green light' your work, as discussed in Chapter 1.2, or it could be the product deliverable to your client.

Depending on your field, the formal presentation is sometimes called **the Review**, **the Critique**, or (in designer slang) **the Crit**. Regardless of its name, it evolved out of studio-based design programs as a way to formally and periodically review an evolving design. At its most formal, it is usually composed of:

- a presenter (the designer),

- a jury (senior designers and stakeholders) who offer a detailed review, and

- an audience that typically includes other designers who are presenting their own work, who may provide additional feedback.

To be effective, your presentation needs to be carefully planned, structured, and rehearsed. As with elevator pitches and desktop reviews, it is your job to make sure your audience understands the problem you are trying to solve, why it is worth solving, and your solution. It is also your job to collect criticisms and feedback from your audience. Because there could be lots going on (and you may be nervous and under pressure), you may want to video record the session so you can review it later, or have a colleague take notes.

References

Parnell, R. and Sara, R., with Doidge, C. and Parsons, M. (2007) *The Crit. An architectural student's handbook*. 2nd edition. Architectural Press.

Pressman, A. 1993. *Architecture 101. A Guide to the Design Studio*. Wiley Press.

YOU NOW KNOW

A critical part of interaction design is about getting feedback about your work as it progresses. This can be done in many forms and at many different times.

- The **elevator pitch** is good for gathering quick reactions to your ideas at any moment.

- The **desktop review** is good for garnering feedback from the people around you, which will likely include colleagues and other people interested in your work.

- The **meeting** is an event planned by you whenever you need feedback, where you can choose who attends.

- The **formal review**, or **crit**, are periodically scheduled sessions where you present and gather feedback about your work from people including decision makers, senior designers, managers, clients, and peers.